Copyright © 2008 by Laura Wall Starke

All rights reserved. No part of this book shall be reproduced or transmitted in any form or by any means, electronic, mechanical, magnetic, photographic including photocopying, recording or by any information storage and retrieval system, without prior written permission of the publisher. No patent liability is assumed with respect to the use of the information contained herein. Although every precaution has been taken in the preparation of this book, the publisher and author assume no responsibility for errors or omissions. Neither is any liability assumed for damages resulting from the use of the information contained herein.

ISBN 0-7414-4945-5

Published by:

1094 New DeHaven Street, Suite 100
West Conshohocken, PA 19428-2713
Info@buybooksontheweb.com
www.buybooksontheweb.com
Toll-free (877) BUY BOOK
Local Phone (610) 941-9999
Fax (610) 941-9959

Printed in the United States of America
Printed on Recycled Paper
Published October 2008

Being the Change

Laura Wall Starke

for my sons

Patrick and Austin

who have their own compelling stories to tell

I am only one, but still I am one;
I cannot do everything, but still I can do something;

And because I cannot do everything,
I will not refuse to do the something that I can do.

Helen Keller

All of us are caught in an inescapable network of mutuality.

Martin Luther King,

Acknowledgments

Writing this book was a joyful experience. It was a privilege to engage in long conversations with compassionate and creative people, who are doing things that matter.

I am sincerely grateful to all who agreed to be interviewed for this book. Thank you for trusting me to tell your story, and for your willingness to share so much, so beautifully, with others.

Thank you to my editor, Barbara Tranin Blank. It was a wonderful collaboration and her belief in the project has meant a lot to me.

Thank you to Carrie Keiser, of the State Wide Adoption and Permanency Network, whose hard work and persistence made it possible for me to interview Josh, the teenager hoping to be adopted, featured in Chapter One.

Finally, I am grateful for the friendship and support I received throughout the year it took to write this book, from my sister Mary Johnston, and friends Aimee Imundo, Bruce Warren, Anne Donato, and of course *The Posse*—Denise D'Addario, Kara McClain, and Lynn Novakoski.

Special thanks to Dave and Darleen Barnett for the loving care they provided my family, and for imparting important lessons on tolerance and acceptance.

TABLE OF CONTENTS

Foreword	1
Introduction	3
Chapter One – Coming Home	5
Chapter Two – Animal Welfare	25
Chapter Three – Overcoming Grief	47
Chapter Four – Building Understanding	63
Chapter Five – Suporting Youth	91
Chapter Six – Music Matters	103
Chapter Seven – Conscious Consumerism	129
Epilogue	149

Foreword

"If you have come to help me, you are wasting your time. If you have come because your liberation is bound up with mine, then come, let us work together." -- Lila Watson, Aboriginal Woman.

If there is a truth in the stories told in *Being The Change*, it is embodied in this not-well-known statement. One cannot read the pages of this book without a growing sense of awe toward the individuals who chose to live their passion, according to their values. In so doing, these remarkable people and their organizations create a rich and vibrant community—one in which art and music is valued, the enrichment of children ensures our future, and creating "homes" for the homeless empowers us. It's a community in which building bridges between and within cultures enhances our well-being and where grief grows into rebirth and renewal--nurturing all parts of creation and bringing wholeness to our universe.

Being The Change gifts us with an inspiring, spiritual and thought-provoking portrait of their work. There is enormous good going on in our communities, which we often miss because of the media's focus on the bad. Emphasizing the latter is what "makes money." The good, however, is the food we need for our souls, our lives, and our communities.

May you enjoy these pages and these stories. May they inspire all of us to "be the change" and live our own liberation.

Tish Mogan
Standards for Excellence Officer
Pennsylvania Association of Nonprofit Organizations,
and a person committed to "being the change."

INTRODUCTION

When accepting the Nobel Peace Prize, Dr. Martin Luther King said "I have the audacity to believe that people everywhere can have three meals a day for their bodies, education and culture for their minds, and dignity, equality and freedom for their spirits."

Every day, people are working diligently, and largely anonymously, to make Dr. King's credo a reality. Being The Change profiles such individuals throughout the region. Some work to provide homes for people without a place to live. Others use art and music as a means of creating community. Still others provide support to those who are disenfranchised, in innovative and often moving ways.

As you read about the quiet efforts undertaken by people in our community, I hope that you will be inspired to join them. At the end of each profile is a section called **Get More Info – Get More Involved**. It provides web addresses, telephone numbers and other information needed for you to participate in the activities profiled in the book.

As nursing student Corey Graham said after her internship working with people with mental illness, "I didn't realize that at first I pitied them. I felt like I was better than they were. It was a very different experience when I stopped observing and started interacting."

The title of the book comes from the words attributed to the Mahatma Gandhi: "You must be the change you wish to see in the world."

Peace,
Laura Wall Starke

CHAPTER ONE

COMING HOME

**Every individual has a responsibility
to our global family.
Good wishes are not sufficient;
We must become actively engaged.**

The Dalai Lama

Introduction

Having a safe place to live is something that most of us take for granted. The reality however, is that many in the region are without a real home. Fortunately several remarkable women are working to change that.

Tina Nixon's organization is providing emergency shelter for women in crisis. Eve Wachhaus's organization literally builds houses for those without them, and Martha Jones and Lorrie Deck are both dedicated to finding loving, permanent homes for teenagers living in foster care, who desperately want to be adopted. While each woman approaches it differently, each is making great strides in providing something fundamental--a place to call home.

WAITING FOR A HOME

Throughout the Commonwealth of Pennsylvania, there are more than three-thousand children in foster care awaiting a permanent home.

Dr. Martha Jones is the Executive Director of Common Sense Adoption. In 1992, Common Sense was the first agency to place a child in an adoptive home under Pennsylvania's new State Wide Adoption and Permanency Network, commonly referred to as SWAN.

SWAN is a partnership between the Commonwealth's Department of Public Welfare, the Pennsylvania Adoption Exchange, and state and private adoption agencies, all working to find permanent homes for children in foster care. Pennsylvania's program is unique, and SWAN administrators are often asked to speak at national conferences.

Martha Jones has worked in the field of child welfare since 1968. She explains that abuse and neglect are the most common reasons that kids end up in foster care. "That means both physical and sexual abuse. It's uncommon to have only one kind."

Although Common Sense Adoption places children of all ages in loving homes, they work primarily with thirteen to seventeen year olds. "It's the age group we see coming up for adoption the most."

According to The United States Department of Health and Human Services, of the over one-hundred-thousand children eligible to be adopted nation-wide, thirty-thousand are teenagers hoping to find a family.

The odds of those teens being adopted, however, aren't good. Lorrie Deck is SWAN's Executive Director. She explains "a child *younger* than nine years old is two times more likely to be adopted than an older child. In Pennsylvania, older kids make up the bulk of those that have no family identified to adopt them."

Nationally, about twenty-five thousand teenagers age-out of the system each year, meaning that they reached the age of eighteen without someone adopting them, and were no longer supported by the foster care system.

Dr. Jones explains "A lot of the teenagers who don't get adopted and age-out end up homeless. Many end up in jail. Many have unwanted pregnancies. And many end up as clients in the welfare system--as parents of children they are now neglecting.

"The problem is these teenagers don't have the support network that a family provides to get them from late adolescence to mid-adulthood," Jones continues. "Even the healthiest child needs help through that. These kids don't generally have the emotional resources, educational resources, or role models to provide that support."

For a teenager without a family, the prospect of adoption can be intimidating. Lorrie Deck recalls "There was an older boy who didn't want to be considered for adoption because he was sure nobody would want him."

SWAN provided the teenager with a dedicated social worker who took him to visit some of his old foster families, and to the middle school that he hadn't seen in years. "He was amazed to see that the families, teachers and guidance counselors all remembered who he was, and were concerned about him. The teenager ended up getting adopted because of services his social worker provided." Deck adds "We have a lot of stories like that."

While many people want to adopt very young children, there are benefits to adopting an older child. Teenagers are able to decide for themselves whether they wish to be adopted, and as a result, are generally ready to be a part of a family.

Martha Jones explains that "Those who have had problems have usually received a lot of counseling and therapy beforehand so they're ready to do their side of it. They're ready to make it work."

Families who are considering adopting a child are required to work with a licensed agency that facilitates the necessary clearances and certifications the family needs. "In terms of eligibility, individuals can adopt. Straight and gay couples can adopt equally. Actually, we have quite a large group of gay and lesbian couples adopting, as well as single parents" Jones says.

Although the need is great, adopting a child from the foster care system is not for everyone. As Dr. Jones explains "There are many, many people who want to adopt and would make wonderful parents, but not for this population."

However, for the right family, teen adoption is enormously rewarding and incredibly important. "I've had families say, 'If we had the money we'd build a bigger house and just keep doing it,' Jones notes. "People who do this best are those who don't have a big hole in their lives. Someone once said 'Two holes don't make a whole.' You have to come to adoption feeling like a pretty strong person and that you have something to offer. I'd rather people were committed than in love. You need the love to get you through, but the commitment is vital."

For those who cannot commit to adoption, there are still ways to be meaningfully involved in a child's life. Teenagers in foster care need mentors. Throughout the country organizations like Big Brothers-Big Sisters of America, and the Boys and Girls Clubs of America operate successful teen mentoring programs. Many work with local foster care agencies.

And as a young person prepares to leave foster care, SWAN works to find an adult willing to be the child's guardian or support person. As Lorrie Deck explains "Maybe that significant person in a teen's lives can't be an adoptive parent, but they can offer somewhere for the child to go over Thanksgiving or Christmas, or if they need to borrow twenty dollars."

SWAN has established a toll-free telephone number for information on statewide resources related to adoption, foster parenting, and supporting teens. And the volunteers staffing the phones are themselves foster and adoptive parents.

Despite the challenges, teen adoptions are often great successes. As Dr. Jones says, "Without their adoptive families, these kids wouldn't have anybody."

Josh

Josh is a slightly built, soft spoken seventeen year old who has spent much of his childhood in foster care. Since he entered the system in 2000, Josh has lived in nine different places throughout Pennsylvania. While he doesn't recall much about it, he liked the first foster home the most. "I don't remember where it was, but I remember that I had so much fun there," Josh says. "It was my favorite one."

Since that initial placement, the teenager has lived in foster homes in Allentown, Bethel, Chester, Harrisburg, Lehigh, Pottsville, and as he explains "more, but I don't remember the other places."

While many kids his age are preparing to graduate from high school, Josh is still a Sophomore. This is not surprising given the amount of moving around he has had to do. "I have no idea how many schools I've been in--at least six, but probably more."

When a child in foster care has to be moved to a new home, efforts are made to keep him or her in the same school. But as Josh's Adoption Specialist, Karen Knodel, explains "if they can't find a placement near the school, there's nothing they can really do."

Josh has been hoping for a permanent home since he entered the foster care system. "I've always wanted to be adopted. It's always been my goal." Having a family would provide the teenager with an important foundation. "For example", he says, "when I'm in college and the other kids go home for Thanksgiving and Christmas, I would have somewhere to go. On college breaks I could go home. Otherwise, I won't really have anywhere to go."

Knodel says that the ideal family for Josh "would be any family that can accept him for who he is, and who is willing to challenge him to become the individual he wants to be."

In early 2007, Josh "came out" as bi-sexual. That admission caused a family that was considering adopting him to change their minds. Fortunately, Josh's current foster family did not have a problem with his admission.

The teenager has become active in his high school's Gay-Straight Alliance (GSA), and enjoys being able to help other students. Josh says, "you don't have to be gay to attend the GSA. A lot of people join the group to support gays and lesbians because they get treated badly in school. Not so much the gay guys, but the lesbians get treated really badly."

Josh has come through his many moves and foster care experiences with an overall sense of optimism. He hopes to find a family that will appreciate his "really good personality, really good sense of humor, and really great hair!"

In fact, when he graduates from high school Josh would like to attend college and major in cosmetology. Someday, the teenager would like to own his own hair salon. And somewhat unexpectedly, the time Josh has spent in foster care may provide him with the people skills needed to be successful in his chosen profession. "Some people would say it's really hard moving around and having to make new friends each time, but I don't really think of it like that. I think of it as a chance to meet more people."

Get More Info – Get More Involved

Common Sense Adoption
800-445-2444
www.csas-swan.org

SWAN Helpline
1-800-585-SWAN (7926)
www.diakon-swan.org

Information on Pennsylvania children available for adoption
www.adoptpakids.org

Big Brothers/Big Sisters of America
www.bbbs.org

Boys and Girls Clubs of America
www.bgca.org

A SAFE PLACE TO LIVE

For more than one-hundred years, the YWCA has provided something essential to women in crisis-- a safe place to live. Tina Nixon understands that until a woman has that, she can accomplish little else in her life.

The YWCA of Greater Harrisburg is often the first agency called upon to support a local woman in crisis, generally through programs offered under the *Housing and Homelessness Services* umbrella.

Nixon has been working to ensure the success of the chapter's programs since 2000, first as the agency's Director of Resource Development and since 2003, as its Chief Executive Officer.

"I'm a doer," says Nixon. "I like making things happen. I live the mission of the Y. This is my life's work."

The agency's Emergency Shelter provides short-term stays of thirty days to women and women with children. The Bridge program provides housing for up to one year, while the Transitional program offers housing for up two years. Both programs help women transition from homelessness to independence.

Women are referred for these and the agency's other services from a variety of sources, including the police and area hospitals. When women arrive at the YWCA, Nixon explains, the agency helps them to get settled in. "Then we start goal planning. We ask 'What do you need to accomplish in order to move forward to self-sufficiency?'"

The women who come to the YW are from all walks of life. Many are living paycheck to paycheck, and many head single-parent households, Nixon explains. "With the majority of them, it's just the luck of the draw." And for some, having a place to live is not the only obstacle to successful independence. Nixon explains "We can find someone a job just like that, but keeping the job is more difficult."

Transportation is a huge issue in Harrisburg, Nixon notes. If a woman has children and no car, she has to pay for transportation as well as child care. "You might live in one area of the city, need to drop off your kids in another, and work in yet another. The buses may or may not cover that."

Helping women to overcome these barriers and achieve self-sufficiency is central to the mission of the agency. "The question we ask here all the time is 'are we enabling or are we empowering?' Many people come to us having been enabled. We want them to leave *empowered*."

Through intensive case management services and hands-on care from staff, the agency helps women succeed. "We tell them, 'If you do 'A,' these are the consequences. However if you make better choices, you are going to be successful.' It's about not being afraid to ask the tough questions."

The YWCA's non-housing services are designed to support women as they find jobs, move into permanent housing, and in the case of many, deal with the effects of domestic abuse. These services include a full-day child development center, before- and afterschool care, life skills classes for adults, and domestic violence and sexual abuse services.

The YWCA of Greater Harrisburg is located at Cameron and Market Streets, at the foot of the Allison Hill section of the city. As Nixon explains, "I was born and raised in this neighborhood. I lived in a house not too far from here. My mother was the type of person who, if you knocked on her door and said you had nothing, she would invite you in and feed you. Whatever she had she would give. I guess I got that from her."

The YWCA's one-hundred-and-twenty-three staff and countless volunteers are equally dedicated to serving the community. Of her staff, Nixon says, "They work hard. They go above and beyond, because they truly believe in the mission.

"As an organization we've got it down when a woman is in crisis and needs shelter and other services. But we also have to focus on the prevention education piece. I really want us to move in the direction of self-esteem building, self-awareness and development."

A prevention initiative that has proved very successful for the YWCA is *Club Ophelia,* an anti-bullying, self-esteem building program for middle school girls created by Dr. Cheryl Dellasega, professor of Women's Studies at Penn State University.

"We first ran the program in the fall of 2006," says Nixon. "It was one of my proudest moments. You know how you do programs and hope for the best? Well, what the kids got out of this was exactly what we were hoping for."

Club Ophelia, a ten-week after school program, served fifteen girls. They participated in role playing and art projects designed to help them understand the dynamics of bullying. The role playing not only included the person being bullied and the bully herself but also the "bystander" who is present but just watches.

"This program is something that is so needed, but usually the community lacks the resources to provide it. Selfishly, I have a son and a daughter who are the age this program targets. I think bullying goes on way too often. I wanted to see the issue start to be successfully addressed."

Club Ophelia also trains high-school girls to act as mentors to middle-school girls. "So it's not us older people telling kids what's what. They can get support and mentoring from kids close to their own age. And it's great for the mentors too."

The fifteen girls who participated in Club Ophelia were referred by various sources. Some live at the YWCA's emergency shelter, while others were referred by their school's guidance counselors. Though fifteen may not sound like a lot of kids, Nixon says it's a "very manageable and interactive number. The girls feel safe and secure so they are able to share. If we did a group with thirty girls we wouldn't be as effective."

A testament to the program's success came in feedback received from parents. "One of the mothers said, 'I haven't been called to school once since my daughter started participating in this program.'"

Club Ophelia enabled the woman's daughter to develop the tools--and the self-esteem--not to lash out at others. "It helped her to use her words, and to understand that her words hurt if she uses them in the wrong way," says Nixon. "This young girl was able to identify the different roles you play in the whole bullying process. I said "Yay! That's exactly what we were trying to do."

As to the future of Club Ophelia, Nixon is cautiously optimistic. The initial goal had been to operate the program year round, serving many more girls. But the cost has been prohibitive. "Hopefully this will become an ongoing, sustainable program. We offered it here on site, but we would *love* to offer it in the schools as well. But you know, you have to take baby steps."

Club Ophelia costs the agency about $5,000 for each ten-week session. Nixon says the YWCA hopes it can keep the program going by finding additional funding.

Managing an agency such as the YWCA of Greater Harrisburg can be difficult, but Nixon explains "I always wanted to do something with my life that had meaning. I wanted to make some kind of contribution to my community."

"Are there challenges? Absolutely." Nixon says, "I hate having to worry about money. Hate it! But it's a job that's never the same. The toilet overflows, the water heater goes out. Who do they call? That would be me."

Then she adds: "Anyone who runs a non-profit knows it's not a nine-to-five job. You can't shut it off and go home. I'm always representing the agency. Even at the Giant. Even at the kids' baseball games. My husband and I used to live not far from here, and it came to a point where clients were knocking at my door. It's hard to separate. It becomes your life."

Get More Info – Get More Involved

YWCA of Greater Harrisburg
1101 Market St
Harrisburg, PA 17103
(717) 234-7931
www.ywcahbg.org

CREATING HOMEOWNERSHIP

How does a person go from homelessness to home ownership?

One way is through Habitat for Humanity. Eve Wachhaus, Executive Director of Habitat's Greater Harrisburg Chapter, says that many of the individuals referred to her agency have no permanent housing and are living in emergency shelters.

To be eligible for a Habitat home, an individual must have an income within 70% of the Federal Government's 'Low and Moderate Income' guidelines, live in substandard housing, and must never before have owned a home.

That means that hundreds of people are eligible to apply for a Habitat house--and the need is great. The agency typically builds six to eight houses a year and would like to increase that to ten. However, each time they're offered, hundreds of people express interest in the workshops that lead to acceptance into the program. While Wachhaus recognizes they cannot serve everyone in need of a home, the agency's reach is significant.

Habitat for Humanity changes neighborhoods as well as lives. It builds houses in one area at a time to maximize the positive effect the new houses will have on a community. As Wachhaus explains. "When we look at locations to build in, we're particularly looking for vacant, blighted, and condemned streets and a willingness by the city or county government to transform those targeted areas into sustainable, mixed-income homes. We build in a single area and transform the neighborhood over time."

The effect of Habitat homes on a neighborhood can be far reaching. The homes not only transform neighborhoods, they build communities. "What's wonderful is that those who are not current home owners see the growth and development of what were once vacant properties. When our volunteer landscapers come out to work, neighbors see what can be done and start to landscape, too. They plant flowers; they mulch. Other families that live on the street start to move along with us. It's very exciting to see the complete transformation of some streets."

Habitat homeowners are full participants in the building of their houses. They take classes in home repair, fiscal responsibility, and street safety. They also help with the construction. Habitat requires 350 hours of "sweat equity" from each person receiving one of their houses.

Ethel Simms is a new Habitat homeowner. "This is a great success for me," she says. "I'm divorced now, and I'm starting all over again. I have three sons. My youngest son is 20 years old, and he still lives with me. My boys are thrilled about this. It's all about patience. You have to be patient. A lot of people get frustrated, but it's all about patience."

Simms has loved helping to build her home and giving back to the organization that made home ownership possible for her. "You have to put in the time. Sweat equity. But in the process, I've had a chance to meet some great people. Everyone has been wonderful. I *love* doing volunteer work for Habitat, and I've passed information on to other people in need. Habitat really works with a bad situation and helps. Habitat gives you hope. And that's a good thing."

Each year, Habitat utilizes the talents of about twenty-four-hundred volunteers, primarily in construction. And in 2006, a group of three-hundred women came together to construct a single house. The project, called *Women Build,* brought together volunteers from all over Central Pennsylvania.

Two of those women are Christine Guss, Habitat's Development Director, and Heather Futato, an agency volunteer.

At the start of Women Build, Habitat's Construction Manager was skeptical about a team of women with no building experience constructing a house. As he worked with the women, however, he changed his mind. Guss relates that eventually the Construction Manager called her to say that the women builders were great. "He said," she recalls, 'They have the best snacks and the best conversations, and they're building a terrific house.'"

The Federated Women's Club of Hershey sent many volunteers, some of whom were over 70. Futato says: "One woman was close to 75 years old, and she was hammering nails like anything. At the end of the day she was really sore, and we asked her, 'Why didn't you just paint?' She answered: 'They asked me to hammer, so I was going to hammer.' And she did!"

"The great thing about Women Build", Futato continues, "is that it encourages women to believe in themselves, because many of the volunteers thought they could *never* do something like this. Women who thought they could not get up on a ladder were up on the roof, shingling. I was doing roofing and found that I loved it. I love being up on the roof."

Many area businesses provided teams of employees to volunteer for the project, including The Limited and Penn National Insurance. Guss recalls a sea of green T-shirts when the insurance company sent several hundred volunteers to the building site.

AmeriCorps, the federal agency that supports volunteer initiatives, helped train workers for the project. As Futato explains, "AmeriCorps was really great about teaching us how to use the equipment--which was key. The agency taught us what to do so when we went to the building site, we were never afraid."

Lowes, the home repair store, also gave classes on using equipment so the volunteers were comfortable with it and with being on a building site, Futato adds.

Hundreds of women working together to build a house was a transforming experience for many. As Guss says, "Everyone who worked on the house found her strengths and abilities. I'd heard the word 'empowerment' before but never saw it in action before this build. People who thought they couldn't do something like this are now doing their own home repairs. They learned not to be afraid."

Habitat for Humanity is making plans to hold another Women's Build.

Get More Info – Get More Involved

Habitat for Humanity
900 S Arlington Ave # 235
Harrisburg, PA 17109
(717) 545-7299
www.harrisburghabitat.org

AmeriCorps
1201 New York Avenue, NW
Washington, DC 20525
www.americorps.org

CHAPTER TWO

ANIMAL WELFARE

The worst sin towards our fellow creatures is not to hate them, but to be indifferent to them. That is the essence of inhumanity.

George Bernard Shaw

Introduction

Each year, local volunteer-run organizations rescue hundreds of abandoned and abused animals. They do this with the help of an extensive network of committed individuals who transport dogs and cats from overcrowded shelters and abusive situations, provide medical care, and foster animals in their homes.

The work the rescue organizations do can be heart-wrenching, but their impact is significant, often resulting in permanent homes for many dogs and cats. And some rescued animals are even giving back to the community.

FURRY FRIENDS

Furry Friends rescues five-hundred dogs and cats every year. Some are strays, some are surrendered by their owners, and others come from overcrowded and dangerous shelters. In a typical year, the organization takes in about 350 dogs and 150 cats.

Remarkably, Furry Friends achieves this through the efforts of only thirty-five people--all of them volunteers. These committed individuals interview potential foster and adoptive families and transport rescued animals to their new homes. They attend public adoption events, work at fundraisers, and sometimes provide foster care themselves.

Robin Scherer, the organization's president and founder, explains that when Furry Friends takes in a dog or cat, it's placed with a foster family while the animal undergoes medical treatment, temperament assessment, and awaits a permanent home.

"When we have a spot in our foster network we take in more animals," Scherer says. "We have some foster families who don't adopt. They just provide temporary homes for animals. Once an animal gets adopted, these foster families take in another."

Scherer herself fosters animals. "It's hard not to get emotionally attached. But I tell myself that if I keep this animal then another one won't have the chance to be rescued. And for every cat that gets saved, there are probably twenty-five others who don't."

For rescue groups to be successful, they must rely on the services of an all-volunteer transport network throughout the country. Transport volunteers will pick up a van load of animals, usually from an overcrowded kill-shelter or puppy mill. They drive the animals to several central locations, where local rescue groups have volunteers waiting to take the dogs and cats to foster or adoptive homes.

While the animals might have to make a multi-state journey, Furry Friends doesn't ask its volunteers to do the same. "To meet a vanload of animals, typically our volunteers will drive about an hour or so, maybe from Harrisburg to Allentown, or from Chambersburg to Hagerstown, Maryland."

Once the rescued animals arrive, they're taken in by Furry Friends' foster homes throughout the area. Two such homes are located in Allentown, but because of limited resources, the organization concentrates on the York/Lancaster/Harrisburg region.

While Furry Friends is completely volunteer-run, caring for five hundred animals isn't cheap--especially when the animals come from abusive situations and may have special needs. "We spend $6,000 to $10,000 each month on vet bills. And that's if we don't have any major fractures or illnesses that come along. It's a huge financial undertaking."

Scherer is grateful to the veterinarians who work with Furry Friends. "We get huge discounts from the vets, typically of 10 to 20 percent. It helps, believe me. If we didn't have that, we'd really be in trouble. We are very grateful to the vets who participate. We really couldn't do it without them."

The discounts, however, only go so far. "We just had a case where six puppies came down with Parvo. In a matter of two weeks we spent about $8,000 to save the puppies' lives."

Parvovirus, or Parvo, is a viral disease that affects dogs. It's especially dangerous to puppies, because the virus prefers rapidly dividing cells. Parvo can be deadly, because it often attacks a puppy's heart and intestinal track."

Furry Friends has established a Hope Fund to help cover the veterinary costs of treating dogs with Parvo or of animals requiring expensive surgery.

To further meet its expenses, Furry Friends holds several fundraisers, including the sale of welcome mats. "They're adorable. They say things like 'Wipe Your Paws.' The mats sell like hotcakes. People love them. They're made by one of our volunteers, and we sell them for $5 each.

"We also have two large annual events," Scherer continues. "*Race For Their Lives* is a 5-K trail run and fun walk that you can bring your dogs to. It's held in September, and we generally raise $11,000 at this event."

Furry Friends is currently hoping to find a D.J. willing to volunteer his or her services at future races.

The agency's other big fundraiser is a Bowl-A-Thon held each spring, called *Strikes For Strays*. Bowlers solicit donations, and Furry Friends provides lunch and prizes. The event generally raises $10,000.

But the money raised doesn't stretch as far as Furry Friends needs it to.

"Our two big fundraising events bring in about two months' worth of vet bills and expenses. The money comes in one hand and goes out the other. Our annual budget is whatever comes in. It really does go right back out."

Scherer founded Furry Friends in February 2001 after coming upon a litter of flea-infested and sick kittens. As she explains, "I started seeing a lot of animals in need, so I decided to do something. My sister-in-law and I worked together on this. We started small and went from there. It's grown to be much more than I ever imagined it would be."

The amount of work involved in running a volunteer organization can be daunting--especially to someone, like Scherer, who also works as a nurse in an area hospital. "It's definitely a full-time job," she says of her work with her organization. "I have two full-time jobs--the one that pays the bills, and Furry Friends. I go home at night and care for my own animals, care for my foster animals, do paperwork, write thank-you letters for donations, post photos of adoptive animals. Everything that a business does, I do. My husband is very understanding."

Most of the organization's adoptions come about as a result of people seeing the animals online. *Petfinder.com* is the website that Furry Friends and many other animal rescue organizations use to showcase their adoptable pets.

While grateful for suitable "forever" homes for their animals, the organization sometimes has to turn down people. As Scherer explains, "These animals have come from bad situations, and we want them to go to ones that are better. We do our best to ensure that the people adopting them are making a lifelong decision.

"We live in a disposable society," she continues. "The most frustrating thing I experience on a daily basis is the lack of human commitment. Our society is disposable in every way, and animals rank low on the totem pole. When someone makes a commitment to an animal, it's a commitment to a living creature that depends on you 100 percent. We allow these animals to be born, force them to be born in the case of puppy mills, and we need to be responsible for their lives."

Although animal rescue can at times be heartbreaking, Scherer remains upbeat. "Even though it can be the most frustrating situation in the world, good often comes of it. We had a dog that was returned to us because she was chewing the furniture. That was all we knew.

"Then we got a call from a veterinarian with the Department of Agriculture, saying that the dog was quarantined because of an altercation with a groundhog. We weren't sure quite what to do. But it turned out that as the vet learned more about Furry Friends, he decided to become a foster home for us. That dog also found a good home with a family that trained her not to chew the furniture."

There are many such happy endings for the animals that Furry Friends rescues, according to Scherer. Here are just a few of them:

<u>A basset hound named Hope</u> – "This was very early on in the existence of Furry Friends. Hope came from a puppy mill. The owners were going to shoot her, because she had a bad leg. Well, that was because they'd picked her up by her leg when she was a puppy, and it had never healed! Hope was adopted, but came down with severe allergies, so the adoptive family made an appointment with the vet to have her euthanized. The vet called Furry Friends to ask if we knew about the situation. We didn't. I called the family and fortunately, they agreed to surrender the dog to us. We were able to find a wonderful new home for Hope. Turns out she's allergic to cats. She's on allergy medication now.

"Even though she had a bum leg, her new family didn't care. They loved her. Her leg ended up having to be amputated, but she's still with her family, and they've given her a wonderful life."

<u>Dudley</u> – "Oh, he's a big black lab. His owners contacted us because they needed to give him up. I couldn't believe it when I saw him. He had hardly any fur at all. It was a combination of allergies and flea infestation. I wasn't sure he'd find a family, but Dudley was adopted by a lovely woman. It wasn't too long afterward that she and her husband split up. Dudley's really been a wonderful companion for her since her divorce. He's helped her a lot. Dudley was allergic to lots of things, but with supplements and allergy shots, all his fur has grown back. It's like velvet now."

<u>Oakley</u> – "Oakley is a little Beagle whose owners dumped him at a rural shelter in West Virginia. He was thrown into a pen with other dogs and almost mauled to death. We rescued Oakley and placed him in a foster home. He had to have his little bandages changed every few hours, and it was touch-and-go for awhile, but he pulled through.

"Oakley was adopted by a wonderful family. He really came around. Now he's a happy little camper. Animals somehow are always thankful for what you do, no matter how badly they've had it."

<u>A Mother Lab</u> – "Several years ago my husband and I were helping repair an animal shelter in central Pennsylvania. A man and a little boy came in with a pregnant black lab. The man made the little boy give up the dog, and oh, the boy just cried and cried. Well, Furry Friends couldn't find a home for the dog right then, but after she had the litter and her seven puppies were weaned, we were able to find homes for the puppies. And the mom found a good home, too.

"About a year later, the woman who adopted the mom arranged to have a reunion. Five of the seven puppies and the mom all got to see each other and play together at a local Dog Park. They had a great time romping and playing. And the adoptive parents became friends. It was great to see how the people were changed because of the animals who had come into their lives."

Get More Info – Get More Involved

Furry Friends
www.furryfriendsnetwork.com

Donations may be sent to
563 Mountain Road
Boiling Springs, PA 17007

To view adoptable pets
www.Petfinder.com

CENTRAL PENNYLVANIA ANIMAL ALLIANCE
and De-Sex In The City

Zella Anderson had been struggling unsuccessfully for years to create a coalition of animal rescue groups in Central Pennsylvania. Then, in October 2003, she attended the *No More Homeless Pets* conference in Philadelphia. The conference was an epiphany for her.

"They preached that rescue groups have to unite because the forces we have to overcome--the puppy mills, the backyard breeders, the pet stores--are a united front," Anderson says. "Unless we band together, we can't compete with them. I spent the whole weekend with 500 people who felt exactly the way I did. I came back inspired."

That inspiration led to the formation of the Central Pennsylvania Animal Alliance. Today, CPAA is a coalition of more than fifty animal rescue organizations working together to help abandoned and abused dogs and cats.

Starting the association was a challenge. "I have to tell you, I didn't really know what I was doing. It's a trial by fire--you just kind of do it and if it works out, great; if not, then try something different."

CPAA decided to focus its resources on purchasing a van for a mobile clinic that would spay and neuter cats in the city of Harrisburg. Anderson explains, "Essentially we believe that the only way we can stop animals from being killed is to prevent them from being born. That's why spaying and neutering are the answer to overpopulation. That's why we're so committed."

It took two years of fundraising, but in 2006 *De-Sex In the City* was launched. To spread the word about the Mobile Clinic, CPAA volunteers went door to door throughout the City of Harrisburg. They went into grocery stores and bars, handing out flyers and telling people about the free spay and neutering program starting in the area.

The clinic typically can operate on twenty-five to thirty cats in one day. "We have three clinics running per month--one for city cats, one at the Harrisburg Humane Society, and, through a partnership with the SPCA of York, one that we take to the trailer parks in that area."

While CPAA asks for donations to help cover its expenses, the organization won't turn anyone away if the individual can't afford to pay for the spaying or neutering.

CPAA also benefits from the assistance of area veterinarians. "We have several vets who help us," says Anderson. "Vets with the Tri County Animal Hospital and Good Hope Animal Hospital run the clinics for us."

The veterinarians are paid a stipend for their work, but also volunteer many hours of their time to this project. The Mobile Clinic runs from eight in the morning until six at night. At each outing one doctor, one vet technician, and multiple volunteers are there to help as needed.

The clinic currently operates only on cats. Because of their smaller size, far more cats than dogs can be operated on in any given period, utilizing fewer resources. Dogs are sent to the VCA West Shore Animal Hospital in New Cumberland or to Noah's Ark Veterinary Hospital in Harrisburg. Both facilities provide their services to CPAA at a reduced rate.

"Our main problem is the lack of vets," says Anderson. The veterinarians working with the Mobile Clinic operate on more than 500 cats a year, which has a significant impact on reducing the stray cat population in the region. But the participation of more veterinarians would mean an even-greater reduction.

To support De-Sex in The City and other programs of CPAA, the organization holds several annual fundraisers.

Compassion In Fashion, a fashion show held each April at the West Shore Country Club in Mechanicsburg, is the organization's signature event. Local stores provide clothing for the models, each of whom is accompanied by a dog who is available for adoption. The canines featured in the fashion show are, as Anderson puts it, "orphaned dogs looking for their forever homes."

The event has been successful on many fronts. It raises several thousand dollars a year for CPAA, and hard-to-place dogs find homes. "We try to include dogs who are older, may have medical issues, or who have been in foster care for a really long time. One of our dogs had been in foster care for several years. Someone who saw him at the fashion show fell in love with him, and he got adopted!"

Woofstock is an annual event that all the rescue groups and animal shelters under the CPAA umbrella participate in. Held at Riverfront Park in Harrisburg, Woofstock provides an opportunity for groups to show off their adoptable animals.

While those wishing to adopt an animal still have to go through an application process, the event has proven very successful in finding permanent homes for dogs and cats. The organizations also sell an assortment of items at Woofstock to help fund their programs.

CPAA recently launched another major program. Hounds For Prison Education, or HOPE, pairs dogs in need of training with men incarcerated at The Camp Hill Correctional Institute.

To participate, prisoners must undergo an extensive screening process, including a psychological evaluation. They cannot have a history of violence or sexual abuse and must have excellent behavior records while in prison. The dogs come from CPAA member organizations and have behavioral problems that make it hard for them to be adopted.

The prisoners are taught how to provide formal obedience training for the dogs, who then receive between six and twelve weeks of training, depending on their needs. The dogs live with the prisoners during this period. The program has been so successful that there's a waiting list for dogs to enter it.

"The goal of HOPE is to train dogs who are not really adoptable and turn them into wonderful dogs that anyone would want to adopt," Anderson says. "The program frees up space at shelters and foster homes at the same time that it gives prisoners something wonderful to do. Several of the prison staff have adopted HOPE animals."

Like most heads of animal rescue groups, Anderson has a day job. She is Senior Litigation Counselor with the Governor's Office of General Counsel. Still, Anderson estimates that she spends about 40 hours or more a week working for CPAA.

"My weekends are totally taken up with it. It just kind of ballooned. I don't know how to explain it, but I've had a soft spot for animals my entire live."

Get More Info – Get More Involved

Central Pennsylvania Animal Alliance
1802 Silver Pine Circle
Mechanicsburg PA 17050
717-732-0611
Email: Adoptions@cpaa.info
www.cpaa.info

PERSONALIZED GREYHOUNDS

Personalized Greyhounds rescues racing dogs who have been retired due to age or injury. Since it was founded in 1995, the organization has found homes for nearly 900 greyhounds.

Louise West is the organization's vice president. She is also the "mother" of Bailey, her own retired racing greyhound and trained Therapy Dog.

When West decided to adopt a greyhound from the organization, she let them know that she didn't have a preference as to the color or size of the dog. "The director called and said, 'Well, I have a dog for you, but he's a *big* dog.'

Bailey is an unusually large greyhound weighing close to 100 pounds, but he has a calm, gentle temperament. Bailey's beige coloring makes him look remarkably like a deer. West explains, "The way Bailey is today is the way he walked in my door. He was perfect from day one in terms of being very unassuming and wanting nothing but love."

Bailey's professional name was Bo Bailey Bear. He raced in Orlando, Florida, until he was retired at three. Racing dogs typically begin their careers when they are eighteen months old and are retired when they reach three to five years.

During his career Bailey won two races, but, as West says, "He prefers retirement. Right now the most exercise he gets is when he's dreaming. He chases bunnies in his sleep."

Historically, racing dogs have been a commodity. When they made money for their owners, they were valued. When they no longer made money, they were discarded.

"When Personalized Greyhounds was established, dogs were being euthanized by the thousands. They would get hurt, and the tracks didn't want to spend the money to repair the injuries. Things have really gotten better. The racing industry has gotten a lot better. We partner with them now."

Many of the groups rescuing greyhounds are in Florida, where the majority of the dog tracks are located. Some rescue groups even operate kennels at the race track. While things have improved for racing dogs, Personalized Greyhounds still sees animals who are sick and injured. "We recently took in a small female greyhound. When this poor girl came in she was in bad shape. She had a leg injury. She had lost eight teeth. She was grossly underweight. She's getting better, but it's going to take some time. Luckily she's in a foster home with a vet."

Personalized Greyhounds takes its role in animal adoption seriously. The organization works hard to find the right permanent homes for the dogs in its care.

"When you make a commitment to adopt an animal, it's a lasting commitment--not just until it becomes inconvenient," West says. "That's why we try to educate people. We have advisors that our families can talk with. If the family sees a problem, we don't want them to wait. If we tackle it in the early stages, we can get through it. If we can't provide the answers, we can refer the family to someone who can."

Before Bailey moved to his permanent home with West and her family, he had been in foster care with a woman who took him to her beauty salon every day. Because he had become used to "going to work" and had a gentle temperament, West thought Bailey had the potential to be a Therapy Dog.

At the time, West had been teaching at Harrisburg State Hospital. Her students were hospital residents with severe mental illness.

"I started taking Bailey to the State Hospital not too long after I got him. I knew the patients were very responsive to dogs. My mom used to volunteer at the hospital years and years ago and would take her dog on a casual basis. I got permission to start taking Bailey. I had to jump through a few hoops, but once people got to know Bailey and be around him, it was just magic."

One of West's students at the hospital was terrified of dogs. The first time he saw Bailey he refused to go to class. Little by little, however, he came to love the dog. "Not only did my student come back to class, but he would sit next to Bailey and pet him. Bailey has won over everybody he's been around."

In 2006 the Commonwealth announced that Harrisburg State Hospital would be closing. The process took over a year to complete, and West stayed in her position for as long as possible. She knew that Bailey's presence offered the patients something consistent at a time of significant change. The hospital staff had also come to love Bailey and appreciated his continued presence.

When the hospital finally closed, West and Bailey began working at Aurora Social Rehabilitation Services, an agency providing programs for adults with mental illness.

"When I started coming to Aurora, it was the same thing," West says. "People were a little hesitant at first, because Bailey is such a big dog. But once someone gets to know him and his quiet ways, they're won over. People really respond to dogs, especially people who have nobody in their lives to hug or cuddle with. Dogs are so nonjudgmental and love everybody who loves them."

In order for Bailey to become a registered Therapy Dog, he had to pass a series of temperament and obedience tests and become certified as a Canine Good Citizen. Therapy Dog International tests dogs on twenty different issues--from temperament to following direction. Bailey has the highest level of certification a dog can receive and has performed more than 250 therapeutic visits.

In addition to his "day job" at Aurora, Bailey sometimes visits group homes where some adults with mental illness live. He is often joined by his sibling, Shani, another rescue greyhound. "But sometimes he stays home and only Shani goes. He can only work so many hours, you know."

By all indications, Bailey loves what he does. "Oh, Bailey loves to work. He knows in the morning that he's the only one of our four dogs who is going with me, and will come flying across the couch when it's time to leave. When we pull up at work, he'll start whining. He can't wait to get out of the car. I would say he loves his job. And he works for biscuits."

Bailey is greeted with love wherever West takes him. Laughing, she says, "It doesn't matter if *I'm* there. In fact, one Christmas I got a phone call inviting Bailey to the Christmas party at the State Hospital. I said, 'Well, that's fine, but is it okay if I came too?'"

Bailey has also been invited to a wedding. "I run into people to this day who might not remember me, but they always remember Bailey," West says. "Because these dogs enrich our lives to such a degree, we owe it to them to take care of them. They're an important part of our community."

Get More Info – Get More Involved

Personalized Greyhounds
717-761-3317
email: louise@pgreys.org
www.pgreys.org

CHAPTER THREE

OVERCOMING GRIEF

To close your eyes will not ease another's pain.

Chinese Proverb

Introduction

Grief can be defeating, but it can also be transformative. The individuals who are profiled in this chapter have faced significant personal loss with courage and grace. They ultimately overcame their grief by turning it into a vehicle for helping others.

RANDI'S RACE

In 2003, Nancy Chavez's twenty-eight-year-old daughter, Randi, was murdered. Randi's husband, Brian Trimble, and his friend Blaine Norris were convicted of the crime. The murder made national news, Dateline, Court TV, and was the subject of an independent film.

The Trimbles' marriage had become strained when Randi objected to the amount of money her husband was spending to make what was supposed to be a low-budget horror film with Norris. Trimble had considered divorcing his wife but then confessed to Norris that he wanted to kill her instead. Norris reportedly replied: "I could do that for you." The two men planned the murder for seven months.

On the night Randi was killed, Trimble had dinner with a friend to establish an alibi, while Norris went to the Trimble home and waited for Randi to return from work.

Nancy Chavez explains: "Randi was strangled, and stabbed twenty-eight times. He hurt her bad. He really hurt her bad. I saw defense wounds on her.

"I don't think Brian knew the depths of Randi's love for him," Chavez continues. "Killing her was just a quick fix. That was easy. My daughter loved him. I loved him. It's so unbelievable that at times I think it's just not true. But I know now that there are people in the world who are like that."

Randi Trimble was Chavez's only child. The two were extraordinarily close, living just a few miles from each other and speaking every day. The murder of her daughter left Chavez devastated. Her grief was so overwhelming that for over a year she rarely left her house.

Following the murder, Chavez took an extended leave of absence from her job. However, when she returned to her position with the State of Pennsylvania, she found it difficult to function well. "I couldn't sleep at night. It seemed like forever. I thought I'd never get out of it. I remember going to work and falling asleep at my desk. I'd have to leave meetings to try and wake myself up. I couldn't get my body and my mind in synch. Not sleeping, I was constantly tired. That went on for quite a few years."

Before her daughter's murder, Chavez had been a community volunteer. But, as she explains, "It took me a while to decide to get back into that--and to know that I could actually help someone else."

In 2005, more than two years after the murder, Chavez felt she was ready to be active in her community again--but this time to honor her daughter's memory. Chavez decided to create an event that would tell Randi's story and help keep women safe from domestic abuse and violence. After a few meetings with Deb Donahue, Executive Director of Domestic Violence Services of Cumberland and Perry Counties, *Randi's Race* was born.

Randi's Race would be a 5-kilometer run, held on Mother's Day Weekend. The proceeds would fund domestic violence awareness and prevention programs.

In a matter of four weeks, Chavez and Donahue had put together a committee of volunteers and worked out the details of the race. Both women felt it was important that the event be fun, that children have a chance to participate, and that everyone could bring their dogs.

Adams-Ricci Park, in East Pennsboro Twp., Cumberland County, was chosen as the location for the race because Randi often walked there with her dog, Monique. Chavez had developed close relationships with township police during their investigation of her daughter's murder. Now they helped to secure the necessary permits. "Actually, when I called the following year, they said, 'Nancy, it's an annual event. You don't have to worry about it.' I was really moved by that."

As race day approached, it became clear that Randi's Race would be an event for the entire family--thanks to the volunteer support received. "All of Randi's best friends--from grade school, high school and college--signed up to work at the race. And their children attended too. Randi wanted children, and so her friends' little ones are the grandchildren I'll never have. It really makes a difference to me that the kids get to have fun. They all receive a medal and a bag full of treats."

Randi's Race also became a place for juveniles on probation to fulfill their community service hours. Two agencies in Perry County sent young men to work as volunteers. As Chavez recalled "And boy, did they help! They worked hard. They loved helping."

Chavez took the opportunity to tell these young men about her daughter and what happened to her. And Randi's story made an impression. Chavez hopes the boys will learn how violence changes families in painful and permanent ways.

As plans for the race progressed, the committee members realized they had no idea how much could be raised for a first-time event, so they decided not to set a financial goal. "We felt very strongly that any amount would make a difference," Chavez says. "But I didn't want to disappoint myself, or Deb Donahue. I said to Deb, 'I have an idea in mind, but I don't want to tell you.'

She said, 'I have an idea too, and we'll just keep that to ourselves.'" Both women hoped the event would raise close to $5,000.

At the completion of Randi's Race, Chavez was handed a slip of paper while standing at the podium, so she could announce the amount of money the event had brought in. She was shocked when she read the paper. Randi's Race had raised $14,416. "Both Deb and I began to cry." Chavez recalls. "I just can't tell you how happy I was. And it was all because of Randi. It was very emotional for me. Randi would have been so proud."

Randi's Race has grown each year since that first event. In 2008 it raised more than $45,000 for programs related to domestic violence prevention and support services. Randi's Race is still held each year in Adams-Ricci Park, on the Saturday before Mother's Day.

The success of Randi's Race encouraged Chavez to take on another project in her daughter's memory.

Silent Witness Silhouettes are life-size wooden cutouts in human form, on each of which is written the story of a woman killed by domestic violence. Many carry photos of the murdered woman. The Silhouettes are part of a national project and have been on tour throughout Pennsylvania. They make a deep impression on those who see them.

"I feel very strongly about this," Chavez says. "These murdered women need a voice. I'm Randi's voice, but not everyone has a voice. People do read the information on the Silent Witness Silhouettes when they go on tour."

The Silhouettes, however, are in need of repair. "They're pretty banged up. They're made out of plywood. I want to have them made from a synthetic material so they'll be strong. The Silhouettes tell the victims' stories. I want the victims to have some dignity. When they're on the road, I want Randi's picture to be strong. I want the other women's pictures to be strong."

Chavez is seeking help to create more durable Silhouettes before they go back on tour.

It has been a long journey for Chavez, but her advocacy on behalf of victims of domestic violence has helped her find a new direction in life. She was asked to speak about her daughter's death at Dickinson College in Carlisle, Pennsylvania. "I thought there would be 20 people or so. There were close to 400 students, and there were a lot of young men in the audience. Their invitation to speak helped me heal."

Even now, there are things Chavez finds difficult to manage. "I like to think I trust as many people as I did before Randi was murdered, but it's not true. I'm cautious about who I bring into my life now." Chavez no longer celebrates her own birthday, which is just three days before the anniversary of her daughter's death.

Chavez is thankful, however, for the support she has received. "My family has always been there for me. And so has Greg." Greg Green is Nancy's longtime boyfriend. "Randi was introduced to Greg two months before her murder. He's stayed with me, and supported me, from that day. It's been a long and difficult journey, but he's stayed with me. I'm not good at hiding my emotions. Some days are good days. Some days are not good days. But he's stayed with me throughout."

Chavez is grateful, too, for the way the community has embraced Randi's Race. "It's about people who have faith in moving their communities forward," she says. "You see their faces, and you know that participating in the race has made a difference to them. All I really want to do is make a difference."

Domestic Violence Services

Deb Donahue is Executive Director of Domestic Violence Services of Cumberland and Perry Counties. The agency, which provides extensive support services to victims of domestic violence, is the beneficiary of the funds raised by Randi's Race. The agency operates an emergency shelter and counseling services for women and children, which is funded in part by the annual event.

"The money raised by the race accounts for over fifty-percent of our annual fund raising budget," says Donahue. "It really does make a difference."

Many people are unaware of the domestic violence services available in their communities and don't know where to go for help. Donahue explains "It's important to get the word out. We try to help people get over the stigma of domestic violence. People are often afraid that by asking for help, their families will break up. But that's a misrepresentation of domestic violence agencies.

We want to make sure the individuals are safe. And there will be times when it's not in their best interest to stay. We're not about breaking up families. Really, we're not the end point, but the beginning."

Get More Info – Get More Involved

Randi's Race and Domestic Violence Prevention Information
www.dvscp.org

Domestic Violence 24-Hour Hotline
1-800-852-2102

Silent Witness National Initiative
www.silentwitness.net

WORKING THROUGH GRIEF

Ashley Fieseler is an earnest nineteen-year-old with a self-effacing sense of humor and a bright optimism made more impressive by everything she has been through. When Fieseler was seventeen years old, her mother committed suicide.

Laurie Fieseler had suffered from schizophrenia. She had spent most of her adult life either in Harrisburg State Hospital or living in a group home. In spite of the enormous challenges her illness presented, Laurie managed to be a loving mother to her three children.

"I was her baby," Fieseler says. "I was closest to her and went to visit her the most. As I got older, she wanted me to be her guardian, but she died before I turned eighteen."

Because Laurie was often in the hospital, Fieseler and her brother and sister didn't see their mother very much. "She started going into the hospital when I was two years old. When I was eight, my parents got divorced. So when Mom got out of the hospital, she went to a group home, and I would visit her there."

Fieseler's father stayed with his wife throughout her many hospitalizations until the situation became too difficult for him to manage. Fieseler says with admiration: "Dad believed this was just a hard patch and stayed with Mom for a long time."

Living at the state hospital or in a group home was difficult for Laurie. "Having schizophrenia, but being a Mom too, she sometimes felt isolated. She couldn't see me all the time."

When Laurie Fieseler was doing well, she would live in a supervised apartment, and her children could stay the night with her. "I know she was ill, but one thing I know for sure is that she loved us very much."

Laurie's suicide left her daughter grief-stricken. "For the first few months, I didn't want to do anything," Fieseler says. But eventually, she began to write. Poetry became a way for the teenager to manage her grief and to remember her mother. Within a few months, Fieseler had written over fifty poems.

As a High School senior, Fieseler was required to do a graduation project. She shared her poems with her advisor, who suggested the teenager use them for the project.

"I never planned for it to be a book, but my advisor thought it could be valuable to other people. I never thought my poetry could do something like that. But after that day, I realized I really could accomplish something."

Since then Fieseler has photocopied her book, entitled *All I Have Now Are Birthday Cards,* and distributed close to fifty copies to friends, family, and several non-profit organizations. "My poems are kind of sad, but they get happier at the end."

One of the places Fieseler's poetry was distributed was Aurora Social Rehabilitation Services, an agency that decades earlier had provided services to her mother. Fieseler also sought out a volunteer position with the organization. "My mom only felt okay if she was helping someone. I wanted to do that too."

Aurora's Drop-In Center located in Dauphin County Pennsylvania, provides daily educational and recreational programs for more than fifty individuals with severe mental illness. Fieseler began teaching clients how to use the computer and worked with them on creative writing. She admits she's always had an interest in the mental health field because, "I was always trying to figure out why my Mom was the way she was. I'm still trying to figure that out. It was hard to balance Mom and her illness."

John Robinson is a participant in Aurora's programs and also benefits from Fieseler's volunteer efforts. "Ashley is terrific," Robinson says. "I learned a lot from her about how to use the computer. She's a very good teacher." Robinson adds laughing, "As a matter of fact, without her I'd still be trying to learn to use the computer."

Because of Fieseler's tutoring, Robinson now has an email account he uses to communicate with friends he can't see frequently. Being able to stay connected to friends has helped reduce the isolation he had been feeling. And Robinson has new confidence in his abilities. "I got it down. Thanks to Ashley I know what to do on the computer."

In 2007, Fieseler began attending Harrisburg Area Community College. Her ultimate goal is to obtain a Master's Degree in counseling from Shippensburg University. Since her mother's death, Fieseler has also been attending Suicide Survivors meetings, held at Polyclinic Hospital in Harrisburg, the first Wednesday of every month.

"It's a really great place," she says. "It isn't necessarily where we go to cry. We tell jokes, and we talk about things."

Fieseler has had the support of a loving extended family and was living with her aunt and uncle at the time of her mother's death. "They were there for me. I'm so grateful to them, and to my grandparents. My grandmother is a great person to talk to. She'll always help out anyone in need."

Still, it hasn't been easy. The teenager now lives in a small apartment she shares with her cousin. She struggles to support herself and to pay her college tuition. And she misses her mother. Yet, Fieseler volunteers at Aurora every week. "For me, I just feel better if I'm helping someone. I can't just sit and do nothing."

Fieseler feels strongly that people with mental illness should be seen as individuals, and not be defined by their disease. "When you're schizophrenic, you're living in hell, and you have to live with it every day. I don't want my Mom to be perceived as a bad person. She was ill.

"I want everyone to know people with a mental illness are still really great people," Fieseler continues. "My Mom was a wonderful listener. And she tried as hard as she could. Being ill she could only do so much, and we never expected more from her. She was so accepting. I could do anything, and it didn't matter. She would love me anyway."

Fieseler just wrote a second book, because, as she explains "a lot of people said the first one was too sad and they want to know that I'm happy now. This one is happier."

From *All I Have Now Are Birthday Cards*

I Wish

I wish
      that I can cry
      and scream your name
      just like when I was five
Because as my tears fell
      you ran to me
      you hugged me
      and made my tears stop
Now seventeen
      I cry and scream your name
      but you do not come
Like when I was five

Why did you let go?

Why did you let go?
Let go of life and others
It was not the time
Your eyes still had much to see
Your hands still had much to feel
Your heart still has people to love
Most of all
      you left a daughter.

Presents Not Gotten

I went Christmas shopping
I got my sister a sweater
> my brother a book
> my dad a candle

Then I walked by a stand.
It had a heart with *Mom* on it.
But I couldn't get it.

Breathe For Graduation

Breathe,
> As I put on my cap and gown

Breathe,
> As they call my name
> and I walk across that stage

Breathe
> As I come running with my diploma

I wish you could breathe
> So I could see you smile with tears
> As I put on my cap and gown

I wish you could breathe
> So I could hear you cheer as they call

my name
> And I walk across the stage

I wish you could breathe
> So I can come running into your arms with my

diploma

Get More Info – Get More Involved

Survivors of Suicide Support Group
717-782-2727

American Federation for Suicide Prevention
www.afsp.org

Aurora Social Rehabilitation Services
717-232-6675
www.auroraservices.org

CHAPTER FOUR

BUILDING UNDERSTANDING

To be free is not merely to cast off one's chains, but to live in a way that respects and enhances the freedom of others

Nelson Mandela

Introduction

The African ethic **Ubuntu** holds that to be human is to belong. *I am because we are.* By sharing who we are--our skills, our time, our compassion--our humanity becomes bound to that of others.

This ethic is embodied by the four people who are profiled in this chapter. Although they provide advocacy and support services, their most important work is promoting understanding and acceptance of the diversity that enriches our community.

LGBTQ ADVOCACY

Christopher Donchak began attending Common Roads when he was 18 years old. At the time, he had just graduated from high school and was about to become a freshman at Harrisburg Area Community College. Now, at twenty-three, Donchak is a regular volunteer for the agency.

Common Roads is a non-profit organization whose mission is to support and enhance the well-being of lesbian, gay, bisexual, transgendered and questioning (LGBTQ) youth across Central Pennsylvania.

Donchak has been an advocate for LGBTQ causes since he was a teenager. While still in high school himself, he helped students launch Gay-Straight Alliances in local high schools throughout the region, including The Milton Hershey School, Cumberland Valley High School and Central Dauphin Voc-Tech.

Gay-Straight Alliances (GSA) are student-led clubs, usually based at high schools, where LGBTQ and straight youth meet for activities. They support one another, work on issues such as combating homophobia, and try to promote tolerance and acceptance of all students.

Donchak also helped the GSAs develop mission statements and plan activities.

"My own high school at the time was very homophobic," Donchak says. "We were not allowed to start a GSA."

With the support of one teacher, the students in Donchak's school met briefly. Then the administration disbanded the group on the grounds that it feared for the student's safety.

Since then, the atmosphere at his high school has "changed somewhat," in Donchak's words. There are several teachers now who have said they would support a GSA. The principal at the time has retired. But the high school still has no GSA.

"I ran into my old principal recently at a bookstore and said to him: 'Do you remember me? Chris Donchak, class of '02. That's the year you wouldn't let us have a GSA because you thought there were no gay kids. Well, we're everywhere.' And I walked out the door. I was so proud of myself!"

Yet, throughout the country, the Federal Equal Access Act has been successfully used by students to establish public school-based Gay-Straight Alliances.

The Act states that: "It shall be unlawful for any public secondary school which receives Federal financial assistance, to deny equal access or a fair opportunity to, or discriminate against, any students who wish to conduct a meeting within that limited open forum on the basis of the religious, political, philosophical, or other content of the speech at such meetings."

While at Harrisburg Area Community College, Donchak has continued his activism—and has been elected President of HACC's Allies group. Allies has a similar mission to Gay-Straight Alliances, but the groups are usually based at colleges and universities.

As President of Allies, Donchak coordinated events for National Coming Out Day, which included the college's first-ever drag show. Nearly two-hundred people attended the event, which raised more than $700 for the group's educational and outreach programs. "We had a lot of support from administration and staff. There was no backlash. There were no protestors. Everyone had fun."

Donchak knew that he was gay from a very early age. "I first got an indication when I was 6. When I was watching a love story on TV, I noticed I was more attracted to the man in the story than to the girl. But I didn't come out in grade school. I went to a Catholic school. That caused some issues for me. I would pray to God every night, 'Please don't let me be gay.'"

Donchak did come out to family and friends the day he graduated from high school. His friends said they already knew and that it didn't matter to them. His family, however, struggled with the news. "My parents were in denial. I had to tell my Mom at least four times in the course of two years."

After he graduated from High School, Donchak took a job at a local hospital. His father had worked for years at a different hospital nearby. One day Donchak had the chance to work an extra shift at the hospital that employed his father. But Donchak's father asked him not to.

"He didn't want his supervisor to know his son was gay. I asked my father, 'Are you embarrassed about me?' And he said 'Yes.'"

Donchak paused, and added "It's not an abusive relationship, but if I have a boyfriend, they don't want to meet him. If I have children, they won't want to see them. They don't want that to be a part of their lives. But either they accept me and my partner, or they won't get to see their grandchildren. Hopefully, when I have children, that will change."

Donchak understands how difficult it can be for young people to come out to their families. That's what drives his advocacy work. "My neighbor's son was 18 when he told his parents he was gay. They threw him out, and he had to walk to his boyfriend's house--about twelve miles away. The next weekend his parents had a yard sale and sold all his things: his bed, his clothes, everything."

"The parents of a friend who lived in Lancaster kicked him out of the house after he came out" Donchak relates. "He only had the clothes on his back. I gave him Common Roads' telephone number, and they gave him the money he needed for a month's rent. With the help of Common Roads, my friend was able to make it on his own. There are so many people who don't know about the resources available out there."

Donchak's work in the community has made a difference to many young people. But he takes it all in stride. "I'm just doing what I think is right. I've had a very positive experience with Common Roads and my advocacy work. Chalk it up to being a little naïve, but it never occurred to me that violence could be directed at me because of what I was doing."

Recently Donchak transferred to Penn State Harrisburg. Currently there is no Allies group at the college. But Donchak has already met with the professor who oversees student organizations, who has said the college would be happy to help him start one.

Once he finishes his Bachelor's degree, Donchak plans to pursue a Master's in Gay and Lesbian Studies at Temple University in Philadelphia. There are only three schools in the country currently offering this Master's program. The other two are in California.

"My dream is to start a GLBT Community Center in Harrisburg serving all of Central Pennsylvania. If I could do that, I would really feel accomplished."

Get More Info – Get More Involved

Common Roads
Common Roads: 717-920-9534 (8:30-5:00 M-F)
Helpline: 866-488-7386 (24-hour hotline)
www.commonroads.org

Other resources
www.PFLAG.org
www.gaystraightalliance.org

PAIRWN

Ho Than Nguyen left Vietnam for The United States on April 29, 1975, the day Saigon fell to the Communists.

She fled by boat with her sister and five brothers, the youngest of whom was four years old. Nguyen was twenty. Before leaving her native country, she had been a University student. Now, suddenly, she was a "parent" to six younger siblings.

Nguyen and her family arrived in the United States and settled in Pennsylvania. "I don't know how I did it, but I did it," she says. "With the help of the government, with the help of the community. I worked hard to learn the language and the culture. I put all my brothers and sister through school, got married, put my own kids through school, and just survived. I *am* a survivor."

Nguyen is both a survivor and a champion of her adopted country. "I am really happy here. This is the land of opportunity. If you are willing to work hard and think outside the box, you can do really well. But I saw how hard it was with no knowledge about services here. When I first came to this country I know nothing, but I learned. When I saw newcomers who didn't know what to do, I wanted to give back what I had learned."

In 2001, after years of working informally to help immigrants, Nguyen launched The Pennsylvania Immigrant Refugee Women's Network, or PAIRWN. The organization provides support, advocacy, and leadership training to women newly arrived from other countries.

Referrals come from individuals, community service agencies, hospitals, churches and community groups. PAIRWN has been very successful in linking immigrant women to existing services. "I used what I learned to create this group. It's been working. It's been busy. It's been crazy. But it's working."

When establishing PAIRWN, Nguyen decided to focus only on services to women. She explains: "Many times when we come here as refugees, the woman has no voice. So we concentrated on women."

To those who come to her for advice, Nguyen suggests they do five things: "Find a job, learn English, open a checking account, get your driver's license, and then buy a car--so you can be independent."

Nguyen also emphasizes the need for education. "The really important thing is for the kids to get a college degree. I don't care what degree you have, but get a degree or learn a trade."

When the organization first began, PAIRWN worked primarily with women from Mexico and Vietnam. "Now" Nguyen explains, "we help women from Ethiopia, Ecuador, Columbia, Bosnia, India, Afghanistan, Iran, Egypt, East and West Africa—from pretty much all over the whole world."

Nguyen believes she knows why refugees from so many countries settle in the Central Pennsylvania region. "This area is a good place for kids to grow up. Some of our people eventually settle elsewhere, but many, many stay here."

While there are many challenges in adjusting to a new culture, the most significant one is language. PAIRWN works with Catholic Charities to host English as a Second Language classes--taking an original approach to teaching reading and writing.

PAIRWN runs creative writing classes that encourage women to tell their own stories. Creative writing reinforces the learning of English and grammar, while it helps women process the changes they have experienced in coming to a new country. That was how Nguyen learned to speak English.

When she first arrived, Nguyen attended a creative writing class for immigrants. "Each one of us corrected everyone's work. We got input from the teacher and from the class. People wrote in English, but if they got to a part where they couldn't think of the word in English, they write in their own language, which is beautiful."

In 2007 PAIRWN hosted its first Women's Health Conference. The daylong event featured workshops to encourage personal growth.

One focus of the conference was to teach women how to prepare foods of their home countries using the ingredients available in their new communities. "Women don't know where to go to get the food they know how to cook."

Nguyen believes cooking is an art form all women can participate in. It allows them to remain connected to their home cultures in important ways. In 2006 PAIRWN published a book of recipes submitted by the women the agency works with. The cookbook is unique in that each woman who contributed a recipe also tells the story of why that recipe is important to them and their family.

As Nguyen explains, "Telling their own stories helps women with their minds and spirits. It helps them take charge of themselves. When women write, they have more control. This is what we would like to see. Empowerment."

Nguyen has aided thousands of women through the agency she founded, but she remains very humble. And very happy. Nguyen explains "My father said, 'Every day you need to do one good deed, learn one good thing, and live life as fully as you can--and you will be happy in your life.' That's what I try to do. I'm pretty happy!"

Get More Info – Get More Involved

PAIRWN
P.O. Box 238
Enola, PA 17025
717-433-0900
Email: pairwn@PAIRWN.org
www.pairwn.org

INTERFAITH ALLIANCE
RELIGION AND SOCIETY CENTER

Rabbi Carl Choper is a thoughtful, somewhat shy man whose quiet nature belies his decades-long history of working for social change.

"I don't think I ever stopped and said, 'I'm an activist.'" Choper reflected on this: "Activism versus Quietism. I do want to explore the relationship between contemplative practice and social engagement, because I think contemplative practice is important. But it must not lead to disengagement from society."

From 1990 until 2006, Choper was the spiritual leader of Temple Beth Shalom in Mechanicsburg, Pennsylvania. It was his desire to work for social change that ultimately led Choper to leave his position and take on a new challenge.

In 2006, Choper became the founding director of The Interfaith Alliance of Pennsylvania (TIA-PA) and its sister group, The Religion and Society Center.

TIA-PA has more than two hundred regular contributors and a contact list of five hundred. It is part of a national organization committed to promoting the positive, healing role of religion in public life by encouraging civic participation, facilitating community activism, and challenging religious political extremism. The national organization has close to two-hundred-thousand members from more than seventy-five different religious traditions and beliefs--including individuals who don't align themselves with any religious tradition at all.

By creating The Interfaith Alliance of Pennsylvania, Choper hoped to bring together community members to foster religious tolerance and mutual understanding among people of faith. By working together, members of the organization believe they could respond to instances of injustice and intolerance that may arise in the community.

"There are groups who see religious diversity as degenerate," says Choper. "We want to celebrate diversity. Our organization is about advocacy, which means we take positions and argue positions."

The two sister organizations have a slightly different emphasis. Interfaith Alliance concentrates its efforts on advocacy. The Religion and Society Center facilitates dialogue among people of faith. "Two different coalitions are necessary. One is for coming together and creating dialogue. The other is for getting the message out."

The Religion and Society Center has taken on four issues for debate. *Religion and the Environment* examines the responsibility people of faith have in caring for our planet. *Religion and Society* examines the relevance of religious traditions in modern society. *Tradition and Pluralism* examines how individuals can remain fully grounded in their own religious traditions, and yet fully accepting of others. *Jewish-Christian Dialogue* promotes understanding between these two major religious traditions.

"Our goal is to make these issues understood in the larger society and to reclaim religious traditions from fundamentalists," says Choper. "We are by nature meaning-seeking people. Religion can be a blessing or a curse, but it cannot be ignored. It's important that we affirm, that we claim, these religious traditions for *life*-- not for *death*. If we simply walk away from them"

Choper stresses "then we abandon these traditions to those who are going to use them for death."

"The flame of faith can inspire and enlighten, and it can also burn. And it *has* burned. On September 11th we saw just that: the terrorists were motivated by religion. And they would have said that the Muslims I appreciate aren't true Muslims. It's just like the churches in the 16th century burning dissidents at the stake. It's just like Baruch Goldstein shooting into a crowd of Muslim worshipers in Hebron."

Goldstein, an Israeli, entered a Mosque in Hebron in 1994 and opened fire on Muslim worshippers gathered for Ramadan, killing twenty-nine people.

Choper saw the importance of honest dialogue when in his fifth year as the rabbi of Beth Shalom, he told his congregation that he's gay. "They handled it well," he recalls. "One family left." Chopper added, laughing, "But when you're the leader of a congregation you can't care if there are a few families who are upset. There's *always* someone upset."

Through that experience with his congregation, Choper saw how vital respectful dialogue can be. "What happened was that people really had to take a look at what they thought was right. What they thought a Jewish community should be. And they realized that they were in much more agreement about the issue then they knew. They had feared that *other* people would have a problem."

During college, Choper spent a year in Israel. "It was exhausting, because I was taking 23 hours of courses weekly, but the field trips were wonderful. We'd study historical places and then we'd go there!"

When the year was over, Choper left Israel to travel through Europe, which included a trip to Germany. While in Munich he made the decision to spend Tisha B'Av, the most mournful day of the Jewish calendar, visiting Dachau concentration camp, just outside the city.

Choper had grown up with an acute awareness of the Holocaust. His mother was born in Vienna in 1937. His grandparents fled the country in 1938, going first to Turkey where his grandfather had business contacts and finally to the United States. Few members of his mother's family survived the war.

As a young man Choper began to question his grandmother about their family history in pre-war Austria. "I asked her, 'How did you know to get out and no one else did?' She got *furious* with me. She said, 'People knew to get out! There were lines around the block at the different consulates with people trying to get visas. People were *trying* to get out. There was nowhere for them to go.'"

"She said 'One day I was pushing your mother down the street because we weren't allowed in the park.' And I said, 'Wait. You weren't allowed in the park?' And she said, 'No. There were signs in the park that read 'No Dogs Or Jews.''"

That exchange had a profound effect on Choper. "I realized then, that you don't go from a tolerant society to genocide directly. There are intermediate steps that a society goes though. Step-by-step-by-step. Those are the steps we need to look out for."

Choper explains how the Holocaust challenges traditional assumptions about God. If God is good, how can such evil happen?

"The conclusion I came to," he says, "is that the way of good is *always* pointed out to us. There *is* a difference between good and evil. If there is no good, and there is no evil, then what happened at Dachau isn't evil--and that much I know isn't true."

Choper continues, "When religion points us toward Dachau, then there's really something wrong. Because when you stare into the abyss, you can always see that there is some call to move the other way."

The call to move toward tolerance and justice is why Choper has devoted himself to The Interfaith Alliance and Religion in Society Center. He hopes the two organizations will encourage people "to come together and listen to and learn from each other." Choper hopes it will become a place where people who believe in an inclusive and compassionate society, can work together to make that ideal a reality.

Get More Info – Get More Involved

The Interfaith Alliance of Pennsylvania
P.O. Box 13059
Harrisburg, PA 17110
Email: interfaithalliance@pa.net
www.tia-pa.org

ESATAMOS UNIDOS

Hector Ortiz and his family came to the United States from Ecuador in 1999. They settled in Harrisburg, Pennsylvania where they had friends.

Ortiz has a Ph.D. in International Relations, with a concentration in Human Rights and currently works for the government of Dauphin County, Pennsylvania. His commitment to cultural understanding and to his adopted community led him to create Estamos Unidos, or United We Stand.

Estmos Unidos is a volunteer run, grass roots organization working with the Spanish speaking community throughout Central and Eastern Pennsylvania. "I wanted to help unify the Latino community. While we have the same language, we come from different countries. We have different religions, different cultures, there are differences in the way we think, the way we communicate and celebrate. But these differences are minor compared to our similarities."

Estamos Unidos began with a simple project--a community Christmas party. Ninety children came to the party that first year, most of them from Harrisburg's inner city. Five years later over four hundred children attend the annual event. "To organize a party for 400 people, we need 80 volunteers."

Ortiz's organization also has a picnic in the summer which over six hundred people attend. "We use this event to recognize leaders in our community – pastors, teachers, coaches - the people who don't usually get recognized but who are trying and trying to save our kids in different ways."

"You need two things to succeed--education and relationships" Ortiz says. "The Education Committee is the most important part of our organization. We concentrate on teaching children. Their past is in Latin America but the future is here, so we try to provide cultural programs celebrating both. The children have to be aware of their own past and of their history so they project themselves to the future. In all our events we emphasize this."

Estamos Unidos runs a summer camp with recreational activities for youth, free English as a Second Language classes, and somewhat surprisingly, Spanish language classes. "We don't want the kids to lose their Spanish when they learn English. Some kids don't know Spanish at all. The classes are free. We generally have about twenty-five kids in the class, and not all are Hispanic kids. Some are white. Some are African American. All are kids who want to learn Spanish."

"This is how we live our mission—through cultural awareness, education, life skills, leadership skills. It's all to create independence. The people we work with can help themselves and help others, creating solidarity in the community."

The organization doesn't just work with children. Leadership Training is an important part of how EU hopes to assist the community it serves. Recently the organization launched a new endeavor--The Latino Professional Association.

"When you watch TV you see the stereotypes. You would think everyone in our community is living on welfare and doing drugs. In reality, we have many professionals, people who are investing in and creating community development opportunities." The Latino Professional Association is intended to provide an avenue for established professionals to mentor others, and to organize around issues of importance to the Latino community.

After six years of working to build a stronger and more unified Latino community, Ortiz can see progress being made. "The way we know we are making a difference is that we see the people we help doing well--getting jobs, buying cars, educating their kids. The organization touches the lives of over 3,000 people during the course of the year."

Although busy with the organization he created and his full time job, Ortiz has also opened his home to teenagers in need. In addition to their son and daughter, Ortiz and his wife are foster parents and have raised several teenagers placed in their care.

"We believe there is a space here for everybody. Thank God my wife and I have been fortunate. There have been open doors and so we give back. We believe we are doing what we are supposed to be doing. We are really only concerned about changing one life at a time."

Get More Info – Get More Involved

Estamos Unidos
130 South 13th Street,
Harrisburg PA 17114
Email: eup@estamosunidospa.org
www.estamosunidospa.org

Tina Nixon, CEO, YWCA of Greater Harrisburg

Bailey, the therapy dog

Zella Anderson, CPAA

Nancy Chavez, Deb Donahue, Randi's Race

Ashley Fieseler

Chris Donchak

Rabbi Carl Choper

Hector Ortiz; Estamos Unidos

Janice Black, CEO, Foundation for Enhancing Communities

Barak, Inc., The Mural Project

Andrew Gray, Sean Hoots, Rob Berliner
of Hoots and Hellmouth

Hoots and Hellmouth, in concert in Philadelphia

Ten Thousand Villages, Coffee Plantation, Nicaragua

CHAPTER FIVE

SUPORTING YOUTH

If we don't stand up for children, then we don't stand for much

Marion Wright Edelman

Introduction

For children to fully realize their capabilities and strengths, they must be nurtured. They must have access to books and art and music.

In our region, two men in particular are helping to make that possible. Wendell Murray has created a community-based arts program, providing opportunities for inner-city kids to be creative. Joseph Bedard started a small foundation that provides free books to area children. These two individuals, each in their own way, are providing children with the opportunity to realize the full potential of their talents and develop into healthy adults.

SHARE KIDS BOOKS FOUNDATION

While attending a meeting of the local Rotary Club, Joseph Bedard had a simple but powerful idea. Why not provide books for children without them?

A representative of the Harrisburg Pennsylvania School District had been speaking about the lack of books in their schools and had asked for a donation to purchase them. "I knew Rotary generally gives ten- to twenty-thousand dollars a year to buy kids books," Bedard says. "I thought that was great, but when you buy retail, that doesn't amount to a lot of books. It's probably one hundred books per thousand dollars."

Bedard reasoned that there were tens of thousands of children's books in homes across the region that were no longer being read--sitting on suburban bookshelves collecting dust. "So I started calling large employers to ask if they'd do a book drive. I wanted to get books to kids who wouldn't have them otherwise."

The project was an immediate and almost overwhelming success. "Most large private sector employers said yes to a book drive." In that first year, Bedard collected more than sixty thousand books, which he distributed to elementary schools and Head Start programs throughout Pennsylvania. From that initial project, the *Share Kids Books Foundation* was born.

Bedard, a real estate agent by profession, began his small, private foundation with a significant mission-- "to collect and distribute new and lightly used children's books to kids, to encourage literacy health for children, to inspire kids to reach their potential, and to make a better world."

Publishers destroy millions of books each year, because warehousing them is very expensive. By giving those books to charities and schools instead, Bedard says, "publishing houses get a tax write-off for donating the books, they don't have to pay to destroy them, and they have a chance to build new readers for a lifetime of books."

Random House donates a million-and-a-half books annually. Bedard receives sixty-thousand of them.

Since it was created in 2004, the Share Kids Books Foundation has given away nearly two-hundred-thousand books, to about eighty children's programs and schools throughout the region. Each group has received between fifty- and five-thousand books, depending on the need of the organization.

The logistics of collecting and distributing thousands of books can be daunting. But, especially in the beginning, it was a community effort. First Industrial Realty Trust provided the Foundation with warehouse space to store the books. Jim Novinger, a local businessman, provided a truck and driver to pick up books from a publisher in West Virginia. "Another company gave us a forklift; another gave us pallet jacks and organized the books for the give-away." And "Super Reader" did his part.

Floyd Stokes is executive director of the American Literacy Corporation. On a regular basis, Stokes dons a mask and cape and becomes Super Reader. He visits schools to promote literacy, and many of the books he takes with him on these outings come from Bedard's Foundation.

"He raids my garage all the time," Bedard says. "That's where many of the books are. People go to my garage, and I never see them. I say, 'The door is open. Take what you need.'"

Throughout the region, small, private foundations such as Share Kids Books are having a positive effect on the community. "In our region, family foundations have a big impact," says Janice Black, President and Chief Executive Officer of The Foundation for Enhancing Communities.

While there can be tax benefits to forming what Black calls a donor-advised fund, the real motivation for these foundations is their mission. Black explains: "What a family or individual usually does is decide what kind of an impact they want to make in the community. Locally, most family foundations serve youth in some way, either in education or health, but many also serve the arts."

Bedard believes in the "power of one"--the ability of a single person to make a lasting difference in the community. And he is quick to point out there are many organizations in other communities having an impact similar to that of his own Foundation. "'I've started talking to people, and found it's usually that a single person gets an idea and it grows into something strong. That's the way the story is in each community."

Although he has worked hard to ensure the success of his foundation, Bedard says he's "just a distribution channel."

"Really, my intent is to improve and enhance literacy so that kids can get connected to their purpose in life. For me, it isn't work. It's my passion. If kids can't read, they're unlikely to get connected to themselves and to the world they live in. But if they *can* read, they have the chance to be inspired by something that can connect them to their world."

Get More Info – Get More Involved

Share Kids Books Foundation
email: joebedard@sharekidsbooks.org
www.sharekidsbooks.org

Foundation for Enhancing Communities
200 North Third Street,
P. O. Box 678, Harrisburg, PA 17108-0678
(717) 236-5040
www.GHF.org

American Literacy Corporation
(717) 232-6656
email: superreaders@aol.com
www.superreader.org

BARAK, INC.

BARAK, Inc. is a non-profit community-based arts organization in Pennsylvania that was created, as its mission statement says, "to enrich lives through performing arts that celebrate diversity and stimulate community action, while upholding and reinforcing universal moral principles."

"We're here to break down the walls of division no matter where they exist," says Wendell Murray, BARAK's founder.

The word "Barak" has its roots in Hebrew. While it has several meanings, two particularly spoke to Murray. "Thunderbolt--that's theater. But it also means giving praise to God."

The organization began in 1999 as a faith-based theater company addressing social issues. However, in 2007, BARAK began to shift its emphasis to providing creative outlets for young people. That change came about in response to the increased violence and racial tension Murray was witnessing in the city of Harrisburg.

"I saw hate being generated because people didn't know cultures other than their own," he says. "There's a need for cultures to be in proximity to each other. We might think some people look a little different from us, but what we want out of life is the same."

Murray was especially troubled by violence among young people. He recognized there was a need for programs offering youth something meaningful to do with their time.

"This is a very sports-minded area. Either you're part of the sports world, or you're just over here free flowing, without direction. A lot of young people were free flowing. There was nothing for them to latch onto, except negative creativity, as I call it."

To provide a positive outlet for the city's young people, BARAK developed *Voices of Youth*. With workshops in visual and performing arts, the program offers opportunities for self-discovery and self-expression in a safe and supervised environment. "With Voices of Youth, we work on an alternative to negative creativity" says Murray.

The program was launched in the summer of 2007 and immediately began to immerse young people in the creative process. "We get the kids on stage and say to them, 'What do *you* want to do?' My philosophy is to look at our kids and see where their interests and talents are. Then we help shape them right where they're at."

Empowering young people is an essential part of BARAK's programs. "If you let kids express their talents," says Murray, "then you're saying to them, 'There is worth in what you can create. There is worth in who you are.'"

When setting up creative arts workshops, Murray ensures that the young participants have exposure to professional musicians and artists. "I put money out to make sure we have people who can really work with the kids. I can teach a drama class. But I'm not an artist. I'm not a photographer. There are people around who are, so we make sure we provide that for our kids."

Murray has worked in the performing arts for more than thirty years. He began his career with the Freedom Theatre in Philadelphia, the oldest black theatre company in the nation. A native of that city, Murray moved to Harrisburg in 1992 following a divorce, to remain close to his young son. Having grown up without a father, Murray was determined that his son would not have the same experience.

Voices Of Youth participants worked throughout the summer of 2007, and the result was a showcase featuring BARAK's students who performed original works of music, theatre, dance and poetry. The showcase was held at the Whitaker Center for Science and the Arts in downtown Harrisburg.

BARAK developed a second program for young people that summer. The Mural Project was inspired by Philadelphia's Mural Arts Program, and gave students the opportunity to create works of public art.

Over the course of several months, students worked under the direction of professional muralist Brett Greiman. As Murray says, "Murals are a fascinating medium that appeals to people on so many different levels."

While working on the project, the students took a field trip to Philadelphia to visit that city's extensive collection of public art. "Philly is the mural capital of the world. We took the kids on a tour to let them see what murals are really like."

The field trip showed the students how powerful art can be. "The kids got to see that at one point those neighborhoods were run down, just like theirs are." Murray explains. "They saw how art was able to transform streets--and really, whole communities."

One Philadelphia mural in particular made a deep impression on the young artists. "There were two houses on either side of a lot. On one wall there was a mural of a grandmother quilting. On the opposite wall there was a mural of kids learning how to quilt. The grandmother's quilt ran down the wall, and in the lot between the two murals neighbors had planted flowers that matched the colors of the quilt. At the back of the lot they had built a playground for the kids to play in. It just took all of us out. We told our kids, '*This* is what you guys are doing.' Murals have a lot of power."

The students completed their work in August 2007. The finished works of art are located in Harrisburg's Reservoir Park. The Mural Project had the support of the city, and Harrisburg Mayor Stephen Reed spoke at the unveiling. "So many people now come through the park where our murals are, and everybody stops," Murray says. "Everybody stops."

Despite BARAK's successes, finding money to run its programs has been difficult. "I had wanted a group of twenty kids to participate in the Mural Project. It was very hard to get funding, so we ended up with ten." Smiling, Murray adds, "Well, sometimes we'd have twelve—we slid in a couple of extra kids."

For Murray, this program is vital because he believes art has the power to re-shape the future of young people heading for trouble. "If you're part of this community, you have to react to seeing a seventeen-year-old pick up a gun and shoot another teenager. That's two lives lost. You know how much money it cost to house a kid in juvenile detention for a year? It costs over thirty-thousand dollars. You know how much it costs to do a mural? Five- to ten-thousand dollars."

Murray's goal is to operate his youth programs year-round, providing a safe environment for kids when they are most vulnerable--between three in the afternoon and seven at night.

"We want to fill that gap, so we're hoping to launch a mural program in the schools." So far the cost has been prohibitive, but Murray hasn't given up. "We're still looking for funding."

The organization accomplishes a lot with very little. BARAK's budget is only about twenty-thousand-dollars-a-year. Murray has continued to work full time as a Registered Nurse throughout his leadership of BARAK. "No one gets paid here. We are run entirely by volunteers," Murray explains.

Good things are happening for the organization, after many years of hard work. "When I look at the showcase at the Whitaker and see the benefit to the kids and the way the community received it, I'm thrilled." With the help of committed volunteers and community support, BARAK will continue to grow.

"Community is about pulling together. We need everybody to pitch in to achieve our common goals. You can say it's an upside-down pyramid. It starts with one, and works up to everyone."

Get More Info – Get More Involved

Barak, Inc.
301 Market Street 5th Floor
Harrisburg, PA 17101
717-724-2154
email: info@barakdrama.org
www.barakdrama.org

Mural Arts Program, Philadelphia
www.muralarts.org

CHAPTER SIX

MUSIC MATTERS

If there is something to be changed in this world, it can only happen through music.

Jimi Hendrix

Introduction

"Music inspires community," says Rob Berliner, mandolin player for the band *Hoots and Hellmouth*.

The individuals profiled in this chapter are indeed inspiring community by bringing music to people in important ways. They encourage the talents of young people, link local artists to audiences, and provide access to live performances. What's more, respect is the common thread running through all their work.

GIRLS ROCK PHILLY

At twenty-seven, Beth Warshaw-Duncan leads a busy life. She has a full-time job, is newly married, and in the summer of 2007 launched Girls Rock Philly--a rock and roll summer camp for girls.

As the camp's website explains, GRP's aim is "to bring the Philadelphia area a girls-only, week-long summer camp serving junior rockers ages 10-18. Led by a team of all female instructors and band coaches, girls learn how to play musical instruments, write songs, discover other women in rock, & finesse their on-stage jump kicks."

Because Girls Rock Philly is an all-female environment, Warshaw-Duncan says, "Girls learn their drums from a female drum instructor; they learn guitar from a female guitar instructor. And the entire program is volunteer run. No one gets paid."

Campers came from all over the area. "Girard College offered us their beautiful campus and we offered scholarships to their students." Girard College is a boarding school in Philadelphia for children in grades one through twelve whose guardians or single-parent families have limited financial means to support them.

"The kids at the camp were from mixed backgrounds," says Warshaw-Duncan. "We had a few pairs of sisters and offered a sisters' scholarship. Some were suburban kids from two-parent families; some were kids from Girard College who have no parents or were sent to the school for a variety of other reasons."

"We were asked the question a lot 'I don't know how to play an instrument, can I still come?' And we said 'Of course.' The kids would ask 'But I'm gonna mess up. Is that okay?' My response was 'Yeah. You'll play the wrong note. You'll break a string. You'll break many strings. We have extra.' We stress that you should learn to the best of your ability. And try out your own stuff as well."

Girls Rock Philly's parent organization, Girls Rock Camp Alliance, is based in Portland, Oregon. It provides administrative support and training for those wanting to start camps in new areas.

At the training sessions provided by the Alliance, says Warshaw-Duncan, "We learned how to talk about music, which mikes and which instruments to use. And all the information learned is shared among everyone."

That kind of cooperative learning is a hallmark of GRP. "It's hard to explain the feeling of the camp environment. Everyone really wants to be there. Everyone is respectful. 'You listen to me and I will listen to you and we will work things out'. It's great to be able to teach that positive interaction to the girls in a way that's fun. They write their own songs, they form a band, they work together."

The community helped support the creation of the summer camp. This support came, for example, from Wharton Community Consultants, a program of The University of Pennsylvania's Wharton School of Business, who took on the camp as a community-service project. "They helped us obtain 501©(3) (Federal tax-exempt) status and to get a practice space."

To make it all work, the camp utilized the talents of twenty-five female volunteers, several recruited at the last minute when others dropped out. Two of the last-minute additions, a bass instructor and guitar instructor, were so moved by their experiences at the camp that they signed up to teach the next year.

"We had a lot of volunteers who were professional musicians. A lot of our volunteers have their own bands or are teachers. We also had a lot of Moms, which was great. Things we hadn't even begun to think about they were on top of. They'd say, 'Oh, I brought toothpicks so the kids won't get their hands sticky.' And I'd say, 'I love that you're a Mom.'

"The way we set up the bands was pretty easy," Warshaw-Duncan continues. "On the first day we did get-to-know-you-exercises, and each girl filled out a form with her name, age, and instrument. We observed how the girls were getting along. When the girls went to instrument practice, the counselors compared notes. We put the bands together based more on personality and interests than on skill level."

A drummer was assigned to each band, which had four or five girls. When there was a more advanced guitarist, two guitarists were assigned to that band--a rhythm and a lead--so that the more inexperienced player didn't feel pressure about being the only guitarist in the group.

In addition, every band had a coach to help the group come together successfully. "Some of the band coaches said 'Let's jam for awhile.' Those who weren't professional musicians said, 'Let's talk about who we are and what we like to listen to--what music we *should* write, what music we'd *like* to write.' Everyone had her own approach to it, and every band turned our pretty differently."

The entire GRP program cost only about $10,000, with camp T-shirts and insurance the big-ticket items. To raise the money needed to run the camp, Girls Rock Philly held fundraisers throughout the year. A dance party in early December 2006 helped raise both money and awareness of the program, as did a silent auction held in April 2007. Those events, along with camp tuition, brought in enough money to fund twenty campers.

Going forward Warshaw-Duncan would like to see the camp expand to two or three times its current size, accommodating more girls. "We had twenty campers this time. I'd like to see us with sixty."

Securing a permanent space for the girls to practice in and having camp-owned equipment are next on the agenda. This would enable the bands to continue to play together after summer camp has ended. Warshaw-Duncan continues to receive emails from the band coaches that say their bands want to practice but have nowhere to go.

While she believes there is a lot that needs to be done in order to secure a permanent practice space, Warshaw-Duncan is optimistic that with community support Girls Rock Philly will continue to grow.

The short-term goal for the camp was the end-of-camp Showcase, which featured the girls playing their own music in their own newly formed bands. "We hoped we'd get some people to come out to see the bands play, and we had about *three-hundred people turn out!* It was great!

"The larger goal, however, is for the camp to be able to provide something lasting for the girls, where they feel capable of expressing themselves. We want to bring all of the happiness and confidence that were present in the safe camp environment into their day-to-day lives.

"The camp was a really wonderful, positive, respectful thing. The kids learned important lessons, such as not interrupting other people, allowing them to finish their thoughts. And you can't believe how much of a change it makes both in your understanding of something and other people's attitudes toward you, when you listen to the whole sentence."

Laughing, Warshaw-Duncan adds, "then you get back to regular life and you get to be like the Disrespect Police – 'I don't appreciate how you said that. It wasn't respectful. Let's sit in a circle and talk about it.' But no one ever wants to sit in a circle."

Get More Info – Get More Involved

Girls Rock Philly
P.O. Box 1512
Philadelphia, PA 19105
(215) 789-4879
email: info@girlsrockphilly.org
www.girlsrockphilly.net

THE JEFFREY GAINES SCHOLARSHIP

"I'm pretty much just making my music, and trying to walk gently through the world."

That's how singer-songwriter Jeffrey Gaines explains the personal philosophy that led him to give back to the community. Gaines and his family, in partnership with Harrisburg Area Community College (HACC), created a performing arts scholarship that each year benefits students who have financial need.

Gaines is a recording artist whose self-titled first album was released in 1992, to critical acclaim. A native of Harrisburg and an alumnus of the college, Gaines wanted his scholarship to give students a chance to "express their soul's voice."

Dr. Edna Baehre, President of HACC, believes The Jeffrey Gaines Scholarship has been significant for the student recipients. "It is one of only two performing arts scholarships the college offers--and the only one that is music related."

Harrisburg Area Community College has a long history of supporting arts education. The college has thriving visual and performing arts programs, multiple performance spaces, an art gallery, and the only glass blowing program in the Commonwealth of Pennsylvania.

"HACC's commitment to investing in cultural education is an important part of what any community college should be doing," says Dr. Baehre. "As our Vision Statement says, 'we are a regional resource for cultural and artistic expression.'" Baehre adds that as president of the college "I often ask myself 'what can I do personally as a contributor to the community, and then also what can the college do.'"

While a student at HACC, Jeffrey Gaines benefitted from its arts programs. "I've enjoyed the visual arts--painting and drawing--all through my school days," he says. "But I do find it isn't the same as performing."

Gaines believes that visual artists are, in general, introverts who will create art whether or not it will be seen by anyone. "But a performing artist has a real emotional need, and something inside them requires a reaction from that audience."

The singer-songwriter understands that the emotional vulnerability required to perform can lead a young artist to become discouraged. The scholarship is meant to provide a little extra encouragement and support. "It's the simplest thing I can do. It's as big and as small as helping someone reach the top shelf in a grocery store. 'I can cut your trying time in half. Here, let me.'"

Fans of Gaines have become aware of the scholarship and make donations to the college on his behalf. "Once you get the ball rolling, it really gets going. The scholarship starts to get energy. I hope the trend will continue, so that each year the recipients can receive more and more support."

Whenever his schedule permits, Gaines attends HACC's commencement ceremonies and meets the scholarship recipients. "They have us all seated together. We take pictures together. They give me cards. It's really moving. And for me it's really fun to do. You see all the happy families. I'm generally a performer at events, but on these days I go down and just grab a seat."

The 2007 recipient of the Jeffrey Gaines Scholarship was Vida Joines. The twenty-two-year-old is a straight-A student, who has put herself through school by running her own cleaning business. "The scholarship really helped me because I completely support myself," Joines says. "I'm on my own. Going to school is very important, but it can get pushed to the back burner because there are bills and things. When I received the scholarship, I met Jeffrey, and that was just awesome. I said, 'Thank you so much. You don't know how much this has spurred me on and helped me to realize more of my dreams.'"

Joines comes from a musical family of six children who performed throughout the region as The Joines Band. "My parents had a dream that we would all play instruments and have a little family band" Joines says. "We played bluegrass and country--a little bit of everything. Growing up in a musical family, we all play at least five instruments. I play the piano, the harmonica, the guitar, but mostly the mandolin."

Joines remains grateful for the support of the scholarship--and especially for the encouragement of Gaines. "I'm very thankful that Jeffrey Gaines realized where he came from and how hard it is, and that he gave back. That's what I want to do in the future. I want to give back to people like me, who are struggling just to pay the bills."

Gaines understands that the arts are a fundamental part of a healthy community with a vital role to play in people's lives. "I know this to be true: in the case of high art such as ballet, it bears witness to the best of human ability. The artists bear witness to the dedication and work it takes to get to that level.

"The audience, the community, then goes out into the street having just seen that dedication and they own a little bit of that greatness," Gaines continues. "'The performers on the stage are made of the same stuff that

I'm made of'. They see that if they're true to their aspirations, it can be done. They walk with a little more pride about human ability, and about their own aspirations."

Gaines believes that live music has the same impact. "If you go to see bands or singer-songwriters, you see us reaching for notes, reaching for expression. When an audience hears a band perform live, there's a physical connection created. Your eyes and ears, even your body, picks up the percussive nature of the music. You get pumped up to go out and do your own thing. Through that experience, people can better communicate their feelings to the loved ones in their lives."

Gaines explains that people need that inspiration "or the hope and dream stuff begins to wither and decay a bit, and from that nothing good can come. Really, if we don't have that, hopelessness begins to grow."

The kind of positive interaction that comes from a shared musical experience can impact the entire community, according to Gaines. "I really think there's a ripple effect. It's just like life. If you're out there driving aggressively, you're going to create that in return. I try to walk through the world making a positive impression on the people I meet, and they respond in kind."

Although he was ambitious for rock stardom when he was younger, Gaines's perspective has matured. "You start out with your own interests, in a self-serving way. But if you do it long enough, you see the impact on other people. You get cards and letters. You become affected by *your* effect on them. You realize that it does have an impact on the world you live in. It's beautiful. It can be very rewarding. And it's our job as performers to be heads-up and aware, because you can miss the rewards that are there for you."

For Gaines, it's all about dealing with people and audiences respectfully. And by providing support to young, local musicians, Gaines lives the values he speaks and sings about.

Get More Info – Get More Involved

Jeffrey Gaines
www.jeffreygaines.com

Harrisburg Area Community College
One HACC Drive
Harrisburg, PA 17110
1-800-222-4222
www.hacc.edu

For Scholarship Donation Information
717-780-2416

CONNECTING ARTISTS TO AUDIENCES

How do musicians living and working in our community find an audience? One way is through local radio stations providing airplay for local artists.

WXPN is a member-supported, public radio station based in Philadelphia and owned by the University of Pennsylvania. Roger LaMay is the station's General Manager. "What XPN is all about is connecting artists to audiences," he says. "One of the ways we're sensitive to the local area is in providing access to local artists."

The radio station recently expanded its signal in Central Pennsylvania and can now be heard throughout the region on 88.7 and 99.7 FM, and in Philadelphia on 88.5 FM. But, as LaMay is quick to point out, "This isn't just a Philly station being beamed into Central PA. *We are local to Harrisburg.* Increasingly media is corporate--national or international--so having locally owned media is really important."

LaMay estimates that the station has approximately ten-thousand listeners in the Central Pennsylvania region--about twelve-hundred-and-fifty of who are members making an annual contribution to support the station.

While most public radio stations provide a mix of classical music and news programming, WXPN is different. It is considered an industry leader in non-commercial radio, and plays a mix of rock, roots, folk, and blues music. The station is also committed to playing independent singer-songwriters and local musicians. "Getting air play for local bands is an important part of what we do. We're making it clear to bands that we're interested in them."

WXPN believes that by giving air time to local musicians, the effect will be cumulative. "We're hoping there will be venues in the community that begin to book more XPN-type bands, generating more interest because we're playing them on the radio" says LaMay. "We hope this in some way helps to invigorate the local music scene." Moreover, XPN will be incorporating local bands into local events.

An important way the station provides support to artists is through *WXPN Welcome Events*, or Welcomes. As a service to venues, artists, and audiences, WXPN selects a number of shows it thinks would be of interest to listeners and "gives those shows a little extra promotional support." The radio station publicizes the concerts on the air and gives the featured artists additional airplay.

"We spread the *Welcomes* to a variety of venues around the region," says LaMay. "And we have a presence at those shows--our volunteers are there. They're an extension of the station, so there's personal contact."

The station's management is serious about staying connected to the community. One way it does this is through *Sounding Boards*, meetings at which groups of listeners get to sit down with LaMay, and with Assistant General Manager and Program Director Bruce Warren, to talk about music. The *Sounding Boards* are held throughout the region several times a year.

It's very unusual for listeners to have access to the General Manager and Program Director of a large radio station. And both men are highly regarded in their fields.

Bruce Warren has won numerous national awards, including "Program Director of the Year" several years in a row. LaMay helped oversee construction of the station's new home, with its expanded broadcast and performance space, and under his management WXPN was named "Non-Commercial Radio Station of the Year" for 2006.

LaMay explains, "When Bruce and I went to the *Sounding Boards* in Harrisburg, one of the things we observed was that the people who listen to us treasured us as much, or more, than our Philadelphia listeners--because there were fewer alternatives. There isn't anything exactly like XPN being offered in the region."

Warren adds: "It starts with something really fundamental--people's love of music. You have to start there. XPN fills a need for a lot of people that is not getting filled through commercial radio. We really connect with people through the kinds of music we play."

Warren believes that WXPN has an important role to play in introducing listeners to artists they might not otherwise know about. "There's an enormous trust factor with XPN. Our listeners are willing to embrace different kinds of music they might not if it came to them some other way. It's really about the values of the radio station matching up with the values of the listener."

WXPN's support of emerging artists is not limited to radio play. Warren believes that local concert events are very valuable for an artist's career. "It has a lot of impact when the station can get the community together to experience local bands performing live," he says.

As part of its commitment to bringing live music to its community of listeners, WXPN produces a multi-day music festival every summer. Nearly twenty thousand people attended the event in 2007. "It's a gathering of the tribe, a payback to the community," says LaMay. "It's about bringing as much music to people for as little money as possible."

The Festival is not a fundraiser. "Our goal is to break even," he says. "It averages out to about fifty-cents a band, which is absurdly reasonable. We had a lot of people tell us ticket prices were 'too cheap'--and in fact they were--but we didn't want to raise prices."

The 2007 Festival featured more than forty bands on two stages. Ticket prices for the entire four-day event were $20 for station members and $30 for non-members. The Festival included performances by Fountains of Wayne, Los Lonely Boys, Susanne Vega, and The Smithereens. It also showcased local artists such as Dr. Dog, and Hoots and Hellmouth.

The Festival is in keeping with the station's mission. As LaMay says, "Our role is to be a guide to new and significant music, and the artists who create it. We expose the audience to music that isn't controlled by commercial media, and isn't limited to the few artists who have a massive following."

Warren adds: "If you're a music lover, it gets confusing, because there's a lot of noise out there. We can be the filter, or the curator, which is an important part of the experience."

For most of his adult life, Warren has been connecting people to new music, and supporting the careers of local artists who have something important to share. In addition to his role as Program Director, Warren is a music writer. *Some Velvet Blog* is his online music blog, introducing emerging bands to a wider audience. In 2007 he wrote the book *Wisdom for a Young Musician*, a collection of interviews with well-known musicians and music industry professionals who shared their experiences for the benefit of younger artists just starting out.

"Writers are broadcasters in a way," Warren says. "They have an audience open to receiving information in the same way someone listening to the radio is." His decades-long experience writing about local music has helped many artists gain wider recognition and connect with audiences.

Warren believes that music has always shaped culture, but perhaps now more than ever before. "Music is ingrained in our society in so many ways. And with the iPod it's become a more customized form of expression-- a more articulated form of emotion. You can feel anyway you want to. You're feeling blue, you get some blue songs. You're feeling blue and you want to feel yellow, you put on your yellow songs."

Concerning the radio station that he has worked at for nearly two decades, Warren says: "WXPN really is about the music. The big difference between us and commercial radio stations is that we're driven by a mission and not by the money. The mission is to connect artists with audiences. And, as Roger always says, 'At the end of the day, we only have to make one more dollar than we spend.'"

Get More Info – Get More Involved

WXPN
3025 Walnut Street
Philadelphia, PA 17104
215-898-6677
www.wxpn.org

Some Velvet Blog
www.somevelvetblog.blogspot.com

NEW MUSIC FOR OLD SOULS

Hoots and Hellmouth is a Philadelphia-based band with rock, blues, and gospel influences that plays "new music for old souls." Band members Sean Hoots, Andrew Gray, and Rob Berliner have been playing together since 2005. Berliner is the band's mandolin player. "I also play guitar, bass, piano, banjo, and I sing," he explains. Berliner, who is in his early 30s, has been a professional musician all his adult life.

WXPN has supported Hoots and Hellmouth since the band's inception. They have appeared on the radio station's *Philly Local* show with Helen Leicht, and played at the summer music festivals in 2006 and 2007. Hoots and Hellmouth has been featured on *The World Café* with David Dye, performed for the station's *Free At Noon* concert series, and was WXPN's "Artist to Watch" in July 2007.

"XPN has been really good about sponsoring our shows and putting their name behind us," says Berliner. "They'll announce our shows on the radio as 'XPN Welcomes Hoots and Hellmouth.' That's nice, because a sizeable chunk of our audience, at least locally, is a direct result of XPN listenership."

That kind of support can boost a band's career. "XPN has that kind of gravitas around town, and around the country really, because at this point the station is the predominant voice in its format," he continues. "Everybody looks up to them. Any radio station we go to around the country is taking lots of cues from them. WXPN has had a lot of success as a non-commercial station, which has been completely embraced by the community."

Hoots and Hellmouth's self-titled debut album was released on Mad Dragon Records in April 2007, and the band spent most of the year on tour to support it. Their sophomore record will be released in late 2008.

"We're on tour about 200 days per year—we're on the road pretty much all the time. It's both very hard and very easy. It's hard because you're away from your home. You're away from your cat. The rent's still got to be paid, unless you're couch-surfing. And you can't couch-surf with a cat." Berliner has a calico named Maceo.

"On the other hand, it's good, because we're playing music. We get to see the country." Berliner adds "And I'm not totally disconnected, because I can walk around a strange town as I'm talking to my friends and loved ones. Aside from physical contact, it's easy to maintain relationships---except with the cat. No one wants to put the phone up to her ear."

The band's commitment to making music, however, does come with personal sacrifice. "At this point, we don't really get paid. If there's a little bit of money at the end of the month we divide it up, but I assure you its peanuts. Currently everybody's working odd jobs. But I find myself above water every single month. Sometimes I panic around the twentieth of the month, but the rent gets paid; my health insurance gets paid. I get fed; the cat gets fed."

For Berliner and his band mates, though, the rewards outweigh the sacrifices. "You start going back to places and people like you. People are singing your songs. I hate to sound like that guy who says, 'And it makes it all worth it,' but in a lot of ways, it's true."

For the members of the band, music and community are inextricably tied. This, at least in part, drives their commitment to making music. "Music inspires community," Berliner says. "Historically, it's been a community activity. People passed down information from generation to generation using music. People sing prayers. People sing folk songs. And until about 100 years ago, music was performed by everybody--not just a few people. When a song started, everyone in the room would sing along. It was a very community-oriented thing."

Creating a genuinely shared experience through music is something the band strives for in its live shows. "We try to separate our performances from band-on-stage/crowd-in-the-audience to a more participatory event. It's interactive." In fact, at WXPN's 2006 music festival, several members of the audience unexpectedly joined the band on stage.

Although they travel much of the year, the members of Hoots and Hellmouth stay connected to their home communities in Philadelphia and nearby Chester County, and with local environmental groups.

"We're very involved with the local farming community--'Buy fresh, Buy local," Berliner says. "Everyone has their own personal quest. Ours is the environment. If we're ever given a pulpit, you can rest assured that will be our issue."

The band members take environmental issues very seriously—even carrying a recycling bin in their van when touring the country. "We recycle every single water bottle we come across. We recycle other people's water bottles. But for every one I pull *out* of the garbage, 10,000 go *into* the garbage."

Berliner acknowledges the importance of individual efforts to save the environment, but believes "we're now faced with a time-sensitive problem that is getting exponentially worse. We need someone to stick a broom in the gears of that problem and stop it. All I can do is slow it down a little bit. I've always thought that someone in a position of power has to put themselves on the line and take a stand, because it's the only *real* way to make a difference."

With ties to local farming, the members of Hoots and Hellmouth encourage support of CSAs—Community-Supported Agriculture. CSA farms work in partnership with the community and enable people to buy locally grown produce from small family farms. CSA members pay in advance for a weekly portion, or "share," of the farm's harvest. Because they pay upfront, members also accept the risk if the farm has a bad season.

This partnership provides financial stability for the farmers, while community members receive locally grown, organic produce from a farm they have helped to support.

"There's a CSA in Chester County," Berliner says. "Sean, Andrew and I went there on Share Day, when all the members of the CSA were coming to the farm. We helped pick the produce, then took that week's harvest back to the farmhouse and cooked a big dinner for everyone. The owners invited people from the farm community over, and we held a concert in the barn for about 100 people on a hot, early August night. It was amazing!

"The band's been food oriented from the beginning," he continues. "A lot of times we cook for our gracious hosts— whoever puts us up for the night. Many times we'll say from the stage, 'We need a couch to sleep on. We'll cook for you.' When someone would take us up on the offer, they'd realize we weren't kidding. We were serious, and we'd cook for them."

What does Hoots and Hellmouth hope for in the future? "We want to keep playing as many different places as we can. We want to be able to play a thousand-seat theater, and then someone's backyard, and then a farmer's market, two more nights at a rock club, then someone's porch. That's how we'll reach the most people. That's how we'll stay connected. Once again community becomes the important thing. Our goal is getting into every community we can and playing for as many different people as we can."

The band's dream is also Berliner's. "As for me," he says, "I definitely want to keep that sense of community in all my musical dealings. I want to stay on the road, I want to play good shows, and I want to do good."

Get More Info – Get More Involved

Hoots and Hellmouth website
www.hootsandhellmouth.com

Chester County CSA Information
www.phillychile.com/csalist

Charlestown Organic Farm
www.charlestowncooperativefarm.org

Inverbrook Organic Cooperative Farm
www.inverbrook.com

CHAPTER SEVEN

CONSCIOUS CONSUMERISM

Any fool can make things bigger, more complex, more violent. It takes a touch of genius--and a lot of courage to move in the opposite direction.

Albert Einstein

Introduction

As consumers in a market-driven economy, our money is our voice. How we make our money, and how we spend it, conveys much about our values. It can also have a significant impact on the lives of other people.

Throughout our region, men and women are running businesses with missions that transcend simply making a profit. Instead, these businesses are tied to building a better, more equitable community for all of us. The business owners are interested in connecting people to the land, encouraging an exchange of ideas, and raising awareness about who makes what we consume.

As Eric Papenfuse, owner of Midtown Scholar Bookstore, says "I can't imagine having a business in any other way."

SPIRAL PATH FARMS

When Terra Brownback, and her husband Mike purchased Spiral Path Farms in 1978, they knew nothing about farming. They were both twenty-three years old, newly married, and from suburban Philadelphia. "We didn't grow up on farms." Terra Brownback explains. "When we bought this place back in the '70s, we were part of the Green Movement. Somehow we had a realization about what the human populace was doing to the planet. We wanted to farm to help save the earth."

Spiral Path is a 200-acre organic produce farm in northern Perry County, Pennsylvania. "It's in a beautiful location," Brownback continues. "You know, we were kids when we bought it. It was sort of dumb-luck. Of course we've put a lot of blood, sweat and tears into the farm in the last 30 years. It was really run down when we bought it, but it was the only thing we could possibly afford."

Today, Spiral Path Farm supplies organic produce for much of the region--as well as areas up and down the eastern seaboard. The Brownbacks sell to organic suppliers who provide food to co-ops and restaurants throughout the Northeast.

In addition, the farm is part of the Tuscarora Organic Growers Cooperative, a group of organic farmers who sell to the Washington, D.C., area. The co-op was started by local organic farmers who wanted to work cooperatively, rather than competitively.

"We also supply the local Wegmans' supermarket. We have a diverse operation."

That "diversity" includes operating as a Community Supported Agriculture, or CSA, farm. "CSA is really a movement going on all over the United States and the world," says Brownback. "Farmers in local communities are growing crops for families. With some CSAs you can work on the farm and pay a lower price than people who don't. But my farm is so far away from the general population that we structure it differently."

In the case of Spiral Path Farms, members pay at the beginning of the growing season for a weekly share of the harvest they will receive from May through November. Members pick up their individual boxes of produce at sites throughout the area. More than thirty different kinds of produce are delivered as they are harvested--including heirloom tomatoes, lettuces, sweet corn, potatoes, peppers and chilies, herbs, pumpkin, melons and other fruit.

In each box, members also receive Spiral Path's weekly newsletter. "It's our main outreach. I mostly write about what's going on at the farm. I began to realize that people were being affected by it, because the newsletter was so positive. Really, I was just focusing on the realities of the crops and life on the farm."

Brownback has also begun to recognize her farm's impact on the community. "We found out for instance, that a local physician collects the extra boxes our members forget to pick up and takes the food to a Latino health clinic," she says. The physician distributes the produce to families at the clinic and conducts classes on nutrition. "We weren't even aware that this was going on until he mentioned it. This is the kind of thing we always dreamed of, and we didn't even know was happening."

Becoming a CSA farm has been very successful for the Brownbacks, who started out with twenty-two members and now have eleven-hundred-and-twenty. "It's grown every year since we've started. I think we've grown because we deliver such a good product, but also because of positive networking."

To encourage people to visit the farm, the Brownbacks host several annual events. "It's how we try to connect people to the land. We have events such as pumpkin picking, and strawberry and raspberry pick-your-own. We do get the people and the kids out. Usually we have more than four-hundred-and-fifty people at those events."

Spiral Path Farm is a family-run business, which is unusual in modern farming. "It's a mom-and-pop operation," says Terra Brownback. "We're not a corporation. We're the only owners. Our twenty-one-year-old daughter is a part of the operation now, and we have a ten-year-old daughter coming on. We'll see what happens with the girls. We'll see if they'll stay in farming and keep it going."

Brownback admits she wonders sometimes how two young people from the outskirts of Philadelphia ended up with a passion for farming. "We knew a little bit about gardening, but somehow we got the farming bug in us. We look at ourselves sometimes and say, 'Why do we have this peasant blood running through our veins?' But then, you only have to go back two generations when the majority of us on the planet had peasant blood."

Whatever the reason, to the Brownbacks, Spiral Path is more than just a means to earn a living. "We're planting seeds and feeding people, more than just in their bellies. We want our farming to pay the mortgage, but we have broader goals: We want to connect people to the land. We want to connect children to the land.

"We get exhausted at times, of course," she continues. "But we are very lucky. We have a job that we love. We're trying to give back to the community and to the planet. We don't always succeed in everything in our lives, but our goals are good."

Get More Info – Get More Involved

Spiral Path Farms
538 Spiral Path Lane
Loysville, PA 17047
Phone: 717-789-4433
Email: fresh@spiralpathfarm.com
www.spiralpathfarm.com

Tuscarora Organic Growers Cooperative
www.tog.coop

MIDTOWN SCHOLAR BOOKSTORE

The Midtown Scholar Bookstore is an anomaly among local businesses. It's an independent, family-run, used bookstore that isn't meant to make a lot of money.

Owners Catherine Lawrence and Eric Papenfuse see their store as a place to bring people together for books and music, art and ideas. They provide free exhibit space to local artists and photographers, and they stock the works of regional poets, writers, and musicians--without commission.

The Midtown Scholar Bookstore is not the bread and butter business of the young couple. They also have a thriving online book business serving colleges and universities across the United States and Canada.

Papenfuse explains, "The bookstore is essentially a contribution to the city of Harrisburg. We could just sell all these books online. We have a 50,000 sq.-ft. warehouse that is filled with books. But there's no substitute for holding a book to see if it's right for you."

It's true," adds Lawrence. "With the bookstore we feel as though we're making a difference in our community more than with anything else we've ever done in our lives. We like having something beyond just a normal job. It is part of our mission, to engage the community through books."

From the very beginning Lawrence had a clear vision of what she wanted the bookstore to be. "Our goal was always to create a special space--one that would be a gathering place for people who are interested in books and music. It would be essentially a salon, in a sort of 18th-century sense."

When it comes to stocking their bookshelves, you won't find the latest bestseller at The Midtown Scholar. "We try to emphasize subjects here that are a part of our mission--art and poetry, but also urban studies and architecture, and radicalism," says Papenfuse. "We try to put books in here that we think are meaningful.

"Books are something that have real value," he continues. "When we sell people books, we feel it's an honest, positive exchange, and we reinvest that in more books and other things we can do for the community. It's a business we're proud of. It's connecting with people who are interested in going out into the world and creating community."

In addition to running their businesses, the couple has two small children who can often be found playing among the books. As Lawrence says, "It's wonderful. I can't imagine any other way to be engaged. It's a pretty kid-friendly enterprise. And it's very flexible, much more so than in an ordinary corporate work environment."

The couple extends the same family-friendly, flexible work environment to their staff. And, as Papenfuse says, "We encourage them to develop as individuals, to use the job as a vehicle toward that. That's part of our philosophy; that's why we have such dedicated employees who are out there giving it their all."

Papenfuse and Lawrence moved to Harrisburg, Pennsylvania from New Haven, Connecticut, when Lawrence accepted a job teaching history at Messiah College.

While she enjoyed her time at the college, both Lawrence and Papenfuse were very aware of the poverty and social divisions existing in their adopted city. Their commitment to helping bring about change ultimately led Lawrence to leave her teaching position.

Papenfuse explains: "We were frustrated with teaching not making enough of a difference. It seemed that what we could create with a community bookstore might be even better for transforming the community, and it's worked really well so far. I think we've done an important job in helping break down barriers. We're finding a different way to get transformative ideas into people's hands--by selling books secondhand instead of teaching."

After deciding to open a bookstore in Harrisburg, the couple intentionally sought out underdeveloped areas. "We were looking for a spot that we felt could make a difference to the whole neighborhood," Papenfuse says.

The bookstore is located on Third and Reily Streets in midtown Harrisburg. While the area is currently undergoing a renewal, this was not the case when Papenfuse and Lawrence bought the building in 2002. "Shortly before we came here this was officially declared a 'blighted area' by the city. There was prostitution and drug dealing, all sorts of problems," Lawrence explains.

Papenfuse adds: "One of the things we felt strongly about was that if you give people something that contributes to the community it will be respected and will allow people to look at buildings differently. That was the idea of the mural. The first thing we did, after we put a new roof on the building, was to commission a piece of public art."

The bookstore's mural runs the length of one outer wall of the building. Painted by local children's book artist Stephen Fieser, it depicts life in Harrisburg. "Before we put up the mural, that wall was covered in graffiti," says Papenfuse. "Some people feared our putting a mural up, but we've never had any problems. It speaks to the larger issue that when you create something beautiful and positive in the community it makes a tremendous difference in the way people view and value the community, the urban space. The mural has become a wonderful gathering place. We have outdoor events and concerts and book sales in front of the mural several times a year."

Once a month, too, the Midtown Scholar Bookstore becomes a venue for live music. "We both love music; music that makes you think and contributes to a culture of thoughtfulness--a political culture with music as a vehicle for change," says Papenfuse. "Live music has the ability to reach out and connect with listeners emotionally in transformative ways. An iPod is no substitute for the connection you can make to live performers and fellow audience members. It's about bringing people together in a mutual, shared experience."

Artists have enjoyed playing at Midtown Scholar, which benefits from fine acoustics and a stage in front of a large window overlooking the street life of the city. The intimacy and warmth of the bookstore creates an environment well suited to performances by singer-songwriters.

"We've had some moving concerts in the past," says Papenfuse. "I think in particular of David Wilcox, who had people in tears. Four or five people told him that his music transformed their lives."

It's not just audiences who leave moved by the experience. Lawrence reports that the musicians themselves are often deeply affected. "They leave having had an incredible experience, seeing their songs so well received. Some artists have left in tears because the experience was so moving."

"Live music is a powerful medium," Papenfuse adds. "It's a meaningful discourse which we're engaging in. These are meaningful songwriters. The live music programs have resulted in people feeling more secure, more empowered, more thoughtful."

Expansion plans are under way to add a coffee house to the bookstore. "We'll serve only Fair Trade," says Papanfuse smiling. "Our staff has already made that clear."

Atticus, a bookstore and cafe on the campus of Yale University, served as the model for Midtown Scholar's future coffee house. Atticus is fondly remembered by Papenfuse and Lawrence as a warm and welcoming place that served coffee, tiramisu and black bean soup. Lawrence envisions creating an inviting space where people "come and engage, and stay and debate. We're importing an intellectual café culture that says we want to talk about serious issues."

Papenfuse and Lawrence met at Yale, where both studied 18th Century American and British History. Their educational backgrounds relate surprisingly well to their current undertakings.

"Our field is essentially the American Revolution and the coffee house culture," says Lawrence. "Part of our interest in starting a coffee house comes from the 18th-century coffee house and how it spurred political change in those societies. And how, in a general philosophical sense, the political discussions that take place within communities at venues such as coffee houses, are at the core of democratic change within the democratic process."

Papenfuse adds: "When you put it like that, it seems destined."

Get More Info – Get More Involved

Midtown Scholar Bookstore
1519 North Third Street
Harrisburg 17102
717-236-2665
www.midtownscholar.com

TEN THOUSAND VILLAGES

"There's a growing consciousness in America that we are very excited about. People are more aware of, and care more about, who is making what they're buying--and how those people are treated."

So states Linda Polley, manager of the Ten Thousand Villages store in Mechanicsburg, Pennsylvania.

Ten Thousand Villages is one of the oldest Fair Trade organizations in the country, with more than one-hundred-and-sixty stores throughout North America. They sell jewelry, gifts and home décor made by artisans in more than thirty countries, as well as Fair Trade coffee, tea, chocolate and other foods.

Fair Trade practices enable artisans and farmers to earn a fair wage for their work and help establish standards for working conditions, which includes prohibiting child and forced labor.

Ten Thousand Villages considers several factors when choosing a group to contract with. "For years we've been seeking out the poorest people, those who are unemployable," says Polley. "Seventy percent of our artisans are women in countries where there is no employment for women. We are giving them the opportunity to earn a decent living. And we have a good reach everywhere we're trying to help."

When it contracts with an artisan or farm group, Ten Thousand Villages makes a long-term commitment to the partnership. As Polley puts it, "We're going to be there for you. You can depend on us."

Representatives of Ten Thousand Villages visit the artisans and farmers at least once every two years. "These are people we truly know. We know the history of their products. Sometime we can show you a picture of the person who made the product. These are people we've built relationships with."

Those relationships are respectful business partnerships. "Customers are sometimes confused, thinking Ten Thousand Villages is like a charity. They'll ask 'How much do you send back to them?' But that's not how it works. We purchase the goods outright. When we place an order and have an agreed-upon price, we give them fifty percent up front so they have money to live on while they manufacture the goods for us. When the product is finished, we pay them the rest. We take all the risk for the materials being sold. It's a business relationship. It's not a charity."

The Mechanicsburg store has the distinction of being the very first Ten Thousand Villages store in the United States. It celebrated its fifteenth anniversary in October 2007.

Dave Bauman is a founding member of the store's board of directors and has worked for Ten Thousand Villages corporate headquarters in Akron, Pennsylvania. In 1992, he was on the committee charged with finding a location for the initial store. The committee sent out letters to churches and civic groups throughout the region to gauge their interest in having a Fair Trade store in their communities.

"We looked at large metropolitan areas, such as Philadelphia, Pittsburgh, and Washington, D.C.," says Bauman. "But the strongest interest came from this area. People were saying they would really support a Fair Trade store. There were some genuinely interested people here. I live in this area, and to my surprise, and pride, this was the area that was chosen for the very first store."

Because of the enthusiasm of the community, plans for the store progressed quickly. The first planning meeting was held in June 1992. The store opened for business on October 31, 1992. Since its inception, Ten Thousand Villages in Mechanicsburg has been governed by a board of directors made up of community members.

As a non-profit organization, the store must cover its own expenses. It runs on a very small profit margin and generally ends up with very little left at the end of the year. To keep overhead low, the store operates with only one full-time and two part-time paid staff--and forty volunteers.

As store manager, Polley is very involved in the mission of the organization and is committed to the principles of Fair Trade. "I did a tour in Nicaragua with Equal Exchange and worked in the coffee fields," she says. "It's extremely hard, physical labor. Every bean is picked by hand, rain or shine, when it's harvest season."

Part of the mission of Ten Thousand Villages is to teach people about the importance of Fair Trade. "The only thing they asked of us in Nicaragua was to please go back and educate the American people. All that our artisans want is to be able to feed their children and send them to school. That's what they use the money for."

Equal Exchange, the organization that Polley traveled with, is a Fair Trade organization whose mission is to "build long-term trade partnerships that are economically just and environmentally sound." It is a leading provider of Fair Trade coffees and teas in the United States.

"Equal Exchange is very good about putting money back into the community and ensuring that no child labor is used," says Polley. "Representatives of the organization travel and meet with the co-ops every year."

It surprises many Americans to learn that much of the non-Fair Trade coffee and cocoa beans that we ultimately consume are harvested using child, and in some cases, forced labor.

The International Institute of Tropical Agriculture (IITA) estimates that there are 284,000 children in Cameroon, Ghana, the Ivory Coast, and Nigeria working in hazardous conditions on non-Fair Trade cocoa farms, doing work that includes using machetes and applying pesticides without protective equipment. In 2000, our own State Department reported that in the Ivory Coast "15,000 children between the ages of nine and twelve have been sold into forced labor on conventional (non-Fair Trade) cotton, coffee, and cocoa plantations."

"One of the things we do here is educate people about coffee and other products", Polley states. The coffee house chains that are ubiquitous in our towns have very little Fair Trade coffee available to consumers. "They could do so much for these farmers. Places like Starbucks don't have Fair Trade coffee readily available. You have to request it, and then they'll brew some Fair Trade coffee while you wait."

The international Fair Trade organization Global Exchange states that "Fair Trade farmers sell only about twenty percent of their coffee at a Fair Trade price. The rest is sold at the (significantly lower) world price due to lack of demand. Demand can be created by large corporations selling Fair Trade."

Demand can also be created by the consumer. The amount of brewed coffee sold annually in the United

States is staggering. According to its website, Dunkin Donuts alone serves nearly *one billion* cups of coffee each year. By consistently asking for Fair Trade coffee, consumers can impact corporate behavior.

As Polley states, "The important thing as a consumer is to always look for the Fair Trade label. The companies that are certified are very transparent. As a consumer, you can feel comfortable--and you can drink with a good conscience."

Fair Trade coffee, chocolate and other products can be purchased at supermarkets throughout the region. Wegmans stores not only sell Fair Trade coffee but have a Fair Trade section of the supermarket that sells a variety of products.

"Wegmans is truly trying to provide Fair Trade goods in volume," Polley states. And of course, you can purchase Fair Trade coffee, tea, chocolate and other items at Ten Thousand Villages stores.

"Our store is important because it provides a place for people who are conscious consumers to shop and feel good about what they are doing with their dollars," Polley continues.

Board member Bauman adds: "From a retailing standpoint it might be small, but from where it started and the good that it does, Ten Thousand Villages is huge."

Get More Info – Get More Involved

Ten Thousand Villages, Mechanicsburg
701 Gettysburg Pike
Mechanicsburg, PA 17055
Phone: 717-696-1474
www.mechanicsburg.tenthousandvillages.com

Equal Exchange
www.equalexchange.com

Fair Trade Federation
www.fairtradefederation.org

Global Exchange
www.globalexchange.org

United States State Department Report
http://www.globalexchange.org/campaigns/fairtrade/cocoa/IITACocoaResearch.pdf

International Institute of Tropical Agriculture
2002 Report
http://www.globalexchange.org/campaigns/fairtrade/cocoa/IITACocoaResearch.pdf

EPILOGUE

For a community to be whole and healthy, it must be based on people's love and concern for each other.

Millard Fuller
Founder, Habitat for Humanity

We are responsible for one another.

Because we are inextricably linked to each other, we are inherently responsible for each other—and all other living things on our planet. Although we may not always accept our mutual responsibility, the responsibility remains.

The people profiled in this book embrace their commitment to others. Quietly, diligently, their work is often transformative. But theirs are only a few of the thousands of stories that could be told, and should be told, in communities everywhere.

Community is not passive. A truly just society requires our participation. I encourage you to become involved in shaping your community. There are so many ways to do so. Support a teenager in need. Buy Fair Trade coffee. Foster a homeless animal. Support local artists and musicians. Seek out produce grown in your town. The ways to be transformative are endless…and endlessly valuable.

Jane Addams said "The good we secure for ourselves is precarious and uncertain, until it is secured for all of us, and incorporated into our common life."

We can secure a future for each of us that is based on tolerance and respect, and not on fear. We can do it by working together.

May you have success and joy on your path to Being The Change.

Get More Info – Get More Involved

> **Links to the websites of many organizations profiled in this book, and more information can be found at**
>
> www.btchange.org
> email: btchange@gmail.com